TO BANISH FOREVER

TO BANISH FOREVER

A Secret Society, the Ho-Chunk,
and Ethnic Cleansing in Minnesota

CATHY COATS

MINNESOTA HISTORICAL SOCIETY PRESS

mnhspress.org

The Minnesota Historical Society Press is a member of the Association of University Presses.

Manufactured in the United States of America

10 9 8 7 6 5 4 3 2

♾ The paper used in this publication meets the minimum requirements of the American National Standard for Information Sciences – Permanence for Printed Library Materials, ANSI Z39.48-1984.

International Standard Book Number
ISBN: 978-1-68134-255-9 (paper)
ISBN: 978-1-68134-256-6 (e-book)

Library of Congress Control Number: 2023945531

THIS BOOK IS DEDICATED TO MATTHEW H. NORTHRUP, Miskogiizhik (1970-2023). Matthew was among my first readers and advisors for this project. He was a longtime friend and my classmate in graduate school. He was a scholar, historian, educator, veteran, father, brother, son, cousin, nephew, and friend. He taught me and many other Minnesotans about Indigenous culture and history, inspiring future generations with his knowledge. I will forever treasure the stories and wisdom he shared with me when I last visited him. I hope Matthew's influence on this work is an honor to his legacy.

CONTENTS

An Acknowledgment of Land, People,
and Institutions   ix

1   Introduction: Hidden History Preserved   1

2   The People of the Big Voice   9

3   The Takeover of Ho-Chunk Homelands   19

4   Ho-Chunk Removals in Minnesota Territory   27

5   The Theft of Minnesota and the Call
for Extermination   35

6   Mankato Men and the Secret Society Tradition   55
     Charles A. Chapman
     The Porter Family
     The Barney Brothers
     John F. Meagher

7   The Knights of the Forest   81

8   The Banishment of the Ho-Chunk
from Minnesota   97

9   Ethnic Cleansing and the Forgotten Legacy   107

Acknowledgments   117

Appendixes

A Senate and House of Representatives of the State
of Minnesota, Joint Resolution Relative
to the Sioux and Winnebago Reservations, 1858   119

B "The Knights of the Forest: A Secret History,"
Mankato Review, April 27, 1886   121

C "Ritual," The Initiation Rites and Oath
of the Knights of the Forest   127

D "Removal of the Winnebago Indians," Petition
to the President of the United States and
to the Secretary of the Interior, January 21, 1863   133

Notes   135

Bibliography   149

Index   157

AN ACKNOWLEDGMENT OF LAND, PEOPLE, AND INSTITUTIONS

Ho-Chunk people still live in the State of Minnesota, parts of which have always been their homelands. The call "to banish forever" an entire group of human beings from this state is now replaced with the everlasting "We are still here!"

I recognize that the work of this book and its research is taking place on the homelands of Dakota, Ojibwe, and Ho-Chunk people that were in part colonized by my own great-great-grandparents, who immigrated from five European countries and Canada. The national and local archives, libraries, and museums holding the source material for this work are located on Indigenous lands and contain items that belong to Indigenous people. Some government and non-profit institutions supporting this work still retain control over Indigenous human remains or their cultural objects. The government actors in this history—the States of Minnesota and Wisconsin, as well as the city of Mankato and Blue Earth County—together hold millions of acres of land that were taken from Indigenous people through coercive and fraudulent treaties whose terms the US government did not fulfill. I support the work of Land Back, a movement in North America that seeks to reclaim Indigenous authority over territories that tribal nations claim by treaty.

1 INTRODUCTION:
HIDDEN HISTORY PRESERVED

On May 3, 1968, leaders at Mankato State College held a ceremony to open a time capsule that had lain inside the cornerstone of the university's historic Old Main Building for a century. The capsule had not rested undisturbed: in 1922 the box survived a fire that leveled Old Main. Its contents, transferred to a new container, were sealed again in the rebuilt structure and preserved for the gaze of the future. At the ceremonial opening, the *College Reporter* listed its contents in vague categories: business cards, newspapers, and miscellaneous items. The newspaper did not mention the Knights of the Forest's "Ritual," a four-page pamphlet detailing initiation rites into the secret society and an oath, included with the other documents of 1860s Minnesota.

Mankato citizens had first sealed the time capsule inside the cornerstone of the Old Main Building at the Mankato Normal School on June 22, 1869, during a large dedication ceremony featuring fraternal organizations. Fraternal organizations, which brought men together to pursue common social or political goals and foster business ties, were important institutions in nineteenth-century communities. A procession had traveled down Front Street, the main street in

Mankato. At the parade's end, the crowd of twelve to fifteen hundred people waited to observe a musical performance, a reading of the contents of the time capsule box, and the "laying of the cornerstone according to the impressive ceremonies of the Odd Fellows, conducted by Noble Grand [Sheldon] F. Barney." Cornerstone time capsule ceremonies with fraternal organizations were a common occurrence in the late nineteenth and early twentieth centuries, especially for publicly funded buildings. Many public buildings in Minnesota have contained cornerstone time capsules, including buildings at St. Cloud State University, the Minnesota State Capitol, and the Grand Army of the Republic Hall in Litchfield.[1]

During the 1968 centennial, university leaders considered "whether to put the articles into another corner stone or into the archives of the college." After some debate, they resealed them in another building's cornerstone. But in 1973, after the university sold Old Main and all the other lower campus

Students from Mankato State Normal School in front of Old Main, 1884. *Minnesota State University, Mankato*

buildings, the Mankato State College Archives retrieved the box and added it to the collection. Finally, in 2004, the university archives publicly listed online the original 1869 items from the Old Main cornerstone. Among them was a document titled "Ritual," containing the initiation rite of the Knights of the Forest. This short-lived but influential secret society existed in Mankato and surrounding communities during the early months of 1863, immediately following the US–Dakota War and the execution of thirty-eight Dakota soldiers in Mankato. Its "Ritual" contains the script for its opening ceremonies and initiation rites. The text of the group's membership oath promised to bind the men "together as brothers in common interest" so they could go forth "stronger and braver in the determination to banish forever from our beautiful State every Indian who now desecrates our soil." The organization's goal was to provoke the removal of the Ho-Chunk Nation from its reservation in Blue Earth County and open the reservation to white ownership.[2]

It is quite likely that numerous members of the Knights of the Forest attended the 1869 cornerstone ceremony. Newspaper accounts published decades later allege that many of the area's prominent men were among the group's members; Asa Barney, John F. Meagher, and Charles A. Chapman disclosed their membership, and John J. Porter Jr.'s was featured in his obituary. Other likely members include Asa Barney's brother Sheldon, who presided over the cornerstone ceremony, and John J. Porter Jr.'s father, John J. Porter Sr., who was a vocal advocate for Ho-Chunk removal.[3]

As Mankato's leading citizens locked away the initiation rites and oath in the time capsule that day, marking it as a piece of the city's history worthy of preservation, they also locked away its compelling evidence of Minnesota's unexamined history of hate. No other copies of the document are known to exist. Scholars have recently begun to uncover more details of the ethnic cleansing and genocide of Indigenous people throughout the United States in the nineteenth century. Studies of paramilitary groups, along with research on nineteenth-century secret societies, have shown us that American frontiersmen organized locally on behalf of the nation's expansionist agenda, known as Manifest Destiny, and were often the main drivers of ethnic cleansing. These narratives challenge the idea of "the government" as a sole actor of dispossession. Minnesota's history is no different. Until recently, very few Minnesota historians have presented the history of state removal efforts as ethnic cleansing that was encouraged, organized, and enacted by white settler-colonists.[4]

The initiation ritual of the Knights of the Forest and the oath its members swore were dedicated to a general anti-Indian sentiment and political allegiance, but all firsthand descriptions of the existence and participation in the group center show that it focused exclusively on the nearby Ho-Chunk reservation. These Mankato men were not concerned with the removal of Dakota people from nearby Brown County, which was already assured. The Knights of the Forest organized *after* the Dakota hangings, *after* the government had already taken most of the Dakota people in Minnesota to a concentration camp at Fort Snelling. Even before the Ho-Chunk were moved to the reservation on the Blue Earth River in 1855, most white settlers in Blue Earth County had vigorously opposed the reservation and had advocated, agitated, and organized for Ho-Chunk removal from Minnesota. Furthermore, the group existed only until the federal government forced the Ho-Chunk to leave the state. The men in Mankato took advantage of the postwar racialized rhetoric and settlers' hysteria to push the federal government into finally exiling the Ho-Chunk along with the Dakota.[5]

Following the US–Dakota War in the fall of 1862 and winter of 1863, a statewide call for extermination of "all Indians"

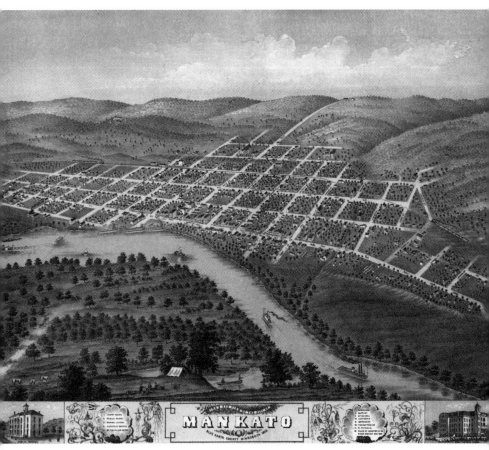

Bird's-eye view of the city of Mankato, Minnesota, in 1870. *Library of Congress*

by white settlers and the threat of postwar mob violence in Mankato was a constant issue for federal and state authorities. Masses of men held "secret meetings" and traveled from New Ulm, St. Peter, and all over Brown County to Mankato, threatening to attack Dakota prisoners. The execution in December publicly enacted and seemed to satisfy the desire for revenge among New Ulm and Brown County settlers who had fought

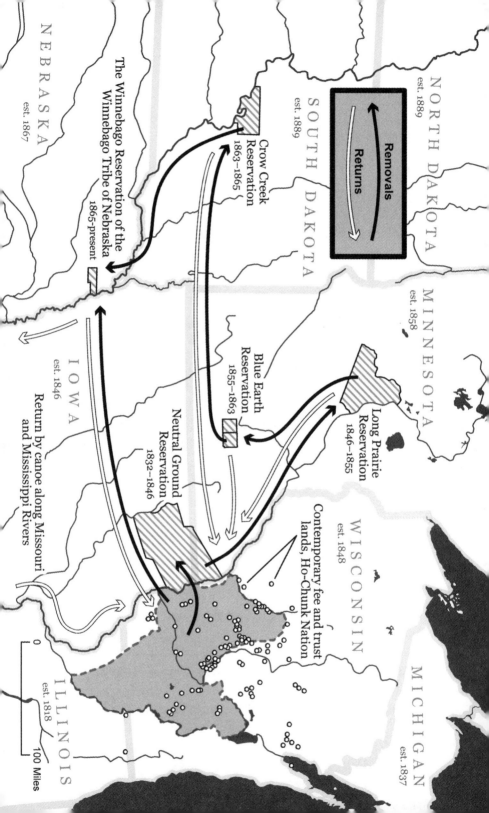

NEBRASKA
est. 1867

NORTH DAKOTA
est. 1889

SOUTH DAKOTA
est. 1889

MINNESOTA
est. 1858

IOWA
est. 1846

WISCONSIN
est. 1848

ILLINOIS
est. 1818

MICHIGAN
est. 1837

The Winnebago Reservation of the
Winnebago Tribe of Nebraska
1865–present

Crow Creek
Reservation
1863–1865

Blue Earth
Reservation
1855–1863

Long Prairie
Reservation
1846–1855

Neutral Ground
Reservation
1832–1846

Return by canoe along Missouri
and Mississippi Rivers

Contemporary fee and trust
lands, Ho-Chunk Nation

Removals

Returns

0

100 Miles

battles with Dakota men close to their homes. But the men of Blue Earth County, who had not experienced conflicts with the Ho-Chunk near their homes, still had the reservation in their midst. Therefore, in January 1863, they organized a campaign for the ethnic cleansing of southern Minnesota.[6]

The Knights' impact on the Ho-Chunk people went beyond their forced removal from Minnesota, however. The Knights of the Forest identified itself as a secret society, but it advanced the agenda typical of a hate group, perpetuating a culture of ethnic violence. Like other hate groups, its members used political power, intimidation, and racial intolerance to promote their cause, but they cloaked themselves in the rhetoric of noble defense. Because of the group's emphasis on secrecy, telling this story requires careful reading of fragmentary evidence. Reasonable suppositions, buttressed with context provided by other secret societies, allow a glimpse of the organization's efforts, members, and effects.

Ho-Chunk people had already attempted a variety of diplomatic tactics before government officials obtained the last of their homelands, so they had a long history of broken treaties with the United States before their arrival in Blue Earth County. The American pattern of deception, colonization, conflict, anti-Indian sentiment, coercion, confinement, and removal was old news to them by the time the US–Dakota War commenced in 1862. Although decades of repeated military roundups had forced most Ho-Chunk people from their homelands at gunpoint, hundreds of families remained in Wisconsin. The blemished and complicated record of the Wisconsin Ho-Chunk removals continued and intensified in Minnesota as American expansion and pre–Civil War discord took hold of the nation. While this history evidently did not matter to the Knights of the Forest, it provides crucial context for this story.

OPPOSITE. Ho-Chunk cessions, removals, and reservations, 1832–present. *Map by Cole Sutton*

2 THE PEOPLE OF THE BIG VOICE

The Ho-Chunk people are indigenous to the areas now known as Wisconsin, Minnesota, Illinois, Michigan, and Iowa. The name they use for themselves is Hochungra, which translates to People of the Big Voice or People of the Sacred Language, a reference to the Ho-Chunk belief that they are the original of all Siouan-speaking people. Nearby Algonquian-speaking people like the Potawatomi and Menominee called them the Winnebago, and Europeans followed suit. Ho-Chunk tradition says their people originated at Red Banks, north of Green Bay, and they have always lived in the area. Their traditional territories range from what we now know as Green Bay to St. Paul, St. Louis, and Chicago. Their population has changed throughout this region, but their ancestral ties to the area have always remained the same. Jean Nicollet, the first European to visit them in 1634, recorded that the Ho-Chunk numbered in the thousands and occupied most of the region that is now Wisconsin.[1]

Over the next few decades following Nicollet's visit, encroachment from northern Algonquian tribes and disease drastically reduced their population. Indigenous people across the Americas were devastated by centuries of successive epidemics after Europeans brought new viruses and bacteria. According to oral traditions and early documents, disease especially affected Ho-Chunk people, possibly because they were concentrated in large communities. Their population and prosperity were on the rebound in the early 1700s when the French began to take an active interest in the area. The Ho-Chunk were reluctant to trade with Europeans, and many engaged in the fur trade only as a side business to their own more successful sustenance patterns of agriculture and hunting. Corn was their main crop and essential to their way of life. They also mined lead for shot and for trade. By the late eighteenth century, Ho-Chunk territory included the area from Green Bay in what is now eastern Wisconsin across the state to Prairie du Chien, Black River Falls, and the lead mining districts of southern and western Wisconsin as well as hunting areas in eastern Minnesota.[2]

Ho-Chunk women held prominent positions of power and esteem in a matrilineal society. They served as the civil-peace chiefs, while men served as military chiefs in a dual leadership system. Hopokoekau, or Glory of the Morning, was a matriarchal leader from the dominant Thunder clan who resided in the modern-day Green Bay area. She maintained stability during the mid-eighteenth century, a period of intertribal wars, early European encounters, and devastating diseases. Sometime around 1830, Hopokoekau married a Frenchman, Sabrevoir de Carrie; they had several children before he left with their daughter. This union inaugurated a dynasty of Ho-Chunk leaders who used a variation of his name, Decora. US leaders insisted on dealing with men, and Hopokoekau's sons and grandsons became prominent diplomats and political leaders, but one of her granddaughters went to Washington to sign a treaty. Hopokoekau's descendants signed every Ho-Chunk treaty with the United States and were perceived by settler-colonists to be "the most powerful of the Winnebago families."[3]

Ho-Chunk women managed day-to-day village work. Men traveled on long hunting trips while women maintained farms, mines, and villages. Ho-Chunk people had been mining lead for hundreds of years as part of their regular seasonal rotation of production, and women were the primary workers of these mines. Women had influence over mining techniques and who could access the mines. When French traders arrived, the women allowed only white men who married Ho-Chunk women to dig. After a favored Canadian trader named Julien Dubuque died in the late eighteenth century, the Ho-Chunk evicted all whites from the mining area except three who were married to Indigenous women.[4]

Since the Ho-Chunk mined lead to exchange for trade goods, they were less dependent on the fur trade than neighboring tribal nations. They hunted more often for subsistence than for market. The mines provided the southern and western bands with economic autonomy for several centuries, which they maintained during the brief era of British presence in their homelands. This lack of attachment to market trade meant the American arrival on the scene in the early nineteenth century was less than welcome. Unlike the British and French before them, the Americans established permanent communities and farms on Ho-Chunk land, continually expanding American settler-colonial society. They also trespassed to mine Ho-Chunk minerals. The American brand of settler colonialism experienced by Ho-Chunk people is characterized by dispossession, adaptation and resistance, and continuing appropriation.[5]

American intention to stay in their homeland likely made Ho-Chunk people deeply uncomfortable. Consequently, some fought alongside the British in the War of 1812 and joined Tecumseh's pan-Indian struggle in order to resist American encroachment. However, once those wars were lost, many Ho-Chunk leaders quickly moved toward diplomatic relations with the United States. Still, some Ho-Chunk bands were rumored to maintain diplomacy at the very same time other groups signed the Ho-Chunk's first "Treaty of Peace and Friendship" with the United States in 1816.[6]

Then, in 1825, the US government brought together a number of Indigenous nations, including Ojibwe, Dakota, and Ho-Chunk, for a treaty council at Prairie du Chien. This treaty was supposed to end disputes over hunting areas by drawing agreed-upon borders, but by creating defined lines between peoples it mostly prepared the way for the United States to sign future treaties for land cessions with each nation. A Ho-Chunk leader named Caramonee told the treaty council that all groups had equal claims to parts of the land and "It would be difficult to divide it—it belongs as much to one as the other." He argued that they held the land in common and no group "had any particular land." Nonetheless, the government created borders between the Ho-Chunk and their neighbors for the first time. Ho-Chunk people had lived along the Mississippi River near modern-day Winona and La Crosse long before Minnesota and Wisconsin Territories existed. But this treaty severed the Ho-Chunk from their traditional hunting areas in what is now eastern Minnesota, and their leaders continued to protest. Some Ho-Chunk people avoided and ignored American intrusion for as long as possible. But for the four decades after those first boundaries were established at Prairie du Chien, Ho-Chunk leaders, like leaders of the other nations, were in an almost constant state of treaty negotiations.[7]

Encroachment and Invasion

As the government became increasingly unable—or unwilling—to stop intrusion and theft by settler-colonists, Ho-Chunks in the lead-mining district found themselves with more and more white antagonists for neighbors. When conflicts occurred between settler-colonists and a few Ho-Chunk people, Secretary of War John C. Calhoun threatened Ho-Chunk leaders with the annihilation of their entire nation. He then held them hostage until they turned over three Ho-Chunk men accused of murdering settler-colonists. On another occasion, Ho-Chunk leaders and American authorities were unable to find Ho-Chunks who murdered a settler family, so an innocent Ho-Chunk man who was in custody, the Boxer, offered his own life in order to save his people.[8]

A series of events in June 1827 brought Ho-Chunk anger over the invasion by American settler-colonists to a boiling point. American miners continued to encroach on the Ho-Chunk lead mines without permission, and an attack on Ho-Chunk women by American keelboat men went unpunished by American authorities. After a contingent of Dakota men misled the Ho-Chunk to believe that the army had executed some of their relatives at Fort Snelling, Ho-Chunk leaders broke diplomatic relations with the United States by not showing up for a treaty council called to draw new borders between several regional tribal nations. Then Prairie du Chien chief Red Bird and a few followers attacked a mixed-ancestry family and an army keelboat. What some historians call the "Winnebago War" or "Red Bird's Uprising" was a small conflict involving a few men. Most Ho-Chunk leaders were attempting diplomatic resolutions, whereas Red Bird diverged with his own solution of direct action.[9]

Nevertheless, panic spread among whites throughout the area. Militias mobilized across Illinois and Wisconsin, where settler-colonists built provisional blockhouses and forts. People in Chicago were terrified that the nearby Potawatomi would join Red Bird. Wisconsin businessman and civic leader General Henry Dodge organized a "Committee of Safety" in Galena, then part of Wisconsin Territory, that later grew into a militia. Territorial Governor Lewis Cass attempted to calm settler-colonists before traveling to St. Louis to request military action. It took nearly two months for General Henry Atkinson's federal army, with the aid of Henry Dodge's militia from Galena, to penetrate Ho-Chunk country in pursuit of Red Bird. As Atkinson moved into the Ho-Chunk homeland in August 1827, Cass revived the treaty council that had been put on hold back in June. Historian Peter Shrake wrote that Cass then "played a shrewd game of psychological warfare" upon the Ho-Chunk Nation, reading aloud dispatches from the army advancement into Ho-Chunk territory to the entire council of several regional tribal nations in an attempt to isolate them from their neighbors.[10]

The lone Ho-Chunk orator at the August 1827 council attempted to maintain the Ho-Chunk Nation's right to the lead mines and received only threats of extermination in return. Chief Four Legs told the government, "We want to know your intentions . . . we are afraid of you." He received his answer the next day when the army threatened to attack the Ho-Chunk "so hard that they will remember it and their children's children." After days of remaining silent while he listened to communications about the army advancing on his people, Four Legs reminded the government that the hostilities had been incited from "your young men at the mines . . . working without our permission," to say nothing of the capture of Ho-Chunk women by army keelboat men. Cass promised to evict American miners, but he added, "You know as well as we do that we must have blood for blood."[11]

As they awaited word of Red Bird's fate, the council turned to the pretenses under which it had originally meant to assemble back in June. The government was concerned with boundary lines between the Ho-Chunk, Menominee, and Ojibwe (although American trespassers were the greatest problem for the Ho-Chunk). Four Legs continued to uphold the Ho-Chunk opposition to needless American-drawn

O'-check-la (Four Legs), head chief of the Ho-Chunk on Lake
Michigan. *Hand-colored lithograph by James Otto Lewis from
the* Aboriginal Portfolio, *painted at the Treaty of Green Bay (1827),
Wisconsin Historical Society, WHI-26879*

intertribal boundaries, saying the new white officials should
"appeal to the ancient traders to say whether they have not
at all times . . . found us hunting as brothers." He then ended
his speech by stating emphatically, "We do not need any line."
Clearly, the Ho-Chunk leader was less concerned with intertribal borders than with American encroachment.[12]

After Waukon Decora and other leaders turned over Red
Bird, US officials coerced them to sign a document allowing

the illegal white miners to remain in the mines until there was a more official adjustment to borders. Ho-Chunk traditions of justice meant they expected Red Bird and his followers to be executed and were dismayed that they instead suffered in prison. One leader told government officials: "We gave them up to you . . . we did so to keep our nation from a war, our women and children from slaughter and to save our country to live and hunt in . . . but now these Indians' lodges are desolate. They are not in the hunting camps or war parties—yet we cannot mourn them—they are not dead." Ho-Chunk leaders then negotiated the release of Red Bird in exchange for permanent ownership of the lead mines. But Red Bird died of illness in prison.[13]

US authorities had led Ho-Chunk leaders to believe that Red Bird's surrender assured there would be no more bloodshed and they could remain in their homeland. Instead, thousands of settler-colonists poured into the mining region after the conflict had ended. Just one year later, at the treaty negotiations of August 1828, the conversation had completely changed. Henry Dodge was now a veteran lead miner. He had stumbled upon a perfect mine while traveling through Ho-Chunk country in pursuit of Red Bird, set up a smelting operation there, and never left. The Ho-Chunk's government agent at the time, Joseph Street, threatened Dodge with military force if he did not leave Ho-Chunk lands. But as more armed miners joined his operation, and the commandant at Fort Crawford—saying the garrison was "undermanned"—refused Street's request to remove them by force, Dodge was able to avoid removal just long enough to have the lines reevaluated so that his claim to the smelting operation was somehow valid. He eventually became governor of Wisconsin Territory and a US senator for the state of Wisconsin.[14]

With local American leaders like Dodge openly setting up mining camps on tribal land, the government and the Ho-Chunk people acknowledged that it was now impossible

Henry Dodge, Wisconsin territorial governor and senator, 1836. *Oil portrait by James Bowman, Wisconsin Historical Society, WHI-2612*

to keep Americans out of Ho-Chunk mines. Their new neighbors were more dangerous than the government. The settler-colonists not only stole their minerals, but they also attacked and abducted Ho-Chunk people. At a treaty council in 1828, one Ho-Chunk leader complained that a group of white men "came and took some of our women, and we could hardly get them back." He added that a young man named Little Elk was nearly killed with a shovel on his way home from trapping. Many Ho-Chunk leaders refused to attend treaty negotiations, and the leaders who spoke at the council avoided making any deals without the proper Ho-Chunk authorities.[15]

Matters would only get worse.

3 THE TAKEOVER OF HO-CHUNK HOMELANDS

As settler-colonists increasingly encroached on Ho-Chunk land, the economic resources of the Ho-Chunk people decreased. One leader, Spotted Arm, asked the government to at least pay for the minerals that whites stole from their mines "so that we may have enough to keep our families warm." Waukon Decora pointedly told a treaty council, "White men are where we need to hunt. Now that there are so many on [the land], we see no game. . . . Do not make us all suffer. . . . What happened last year [with Red Bird] did not come from us." White settlement itself had been detrimental to both the scope of Ho-Chunk hunting grounds and the game population. Government agents agreed with these facts, but they argued that the Ho-Chunk's inability to hunt on the land meant that the land was "more valuable to us than it is to you." Furthermore, the government was not going to pay for small amounts of stolen minerals, because they wanted the entire mine region.[1]

OPPOSITE. Waukon Decora, about 1867. He signed the Treaty of 1855 as "Maw-he-coo-shaw-hoo-no-kaw, One Who Stands and Reaches the Sky, called Little Decorie." On the Treaty of 1865 he is called "Little Dakoria." *Photo by James F. Bodtker, Wisconsin Historical Society, WHI-61421*

The Ho-Chunk leaders successfully resisted a land cession for another year, even though they signed a provisional treaty that ensured its inevitability. Their diplomats stood their ground on several issues, despite the presence of a settler panic after Red Bird's actions. When the Americans drew a map of the Ho-Chunk lead-mining district that they wished to purchase, tribal leaders in attendance all agreed, "The line is not right." They refused to make a final agreement until several of their key leaders could attend a meeting the following spring. A Ho-Chunk leader named Little Priest told government agents he was not going to sell his land or have it "cut up" with borderlines. But according to historian Amy Lonetree, Ho-Chunk leaders were forced to sell the rich lead-mining district in an 1829 treaty "for the shockingly low sum of 29 cents an acre. Even by a conservative estimate, the land was valued at $1.25 an acre."[2]

Just three years later, in 1832, another panic spread among white settler-colonists in Ho-Chunk country during the Black Hawk War. A Sauk leader named Black Hawk led about a thousand of his people, mostly women and children, from Iowa Territory back to their Illinois homeland in defiance of a US removal treaty. The US military enlisted Ho-Chunk soldiers to aid their attacks on the Sauk in parts of Wisconsin. However, other Ho-Chunks were sympathetic to Black Hawk, and some leaders like Winneshiek and White Crow tried to appear neutral. Later that fall, Waukon Decora aided in the surrender of Black Hawk to end the war, a fact that he used for leverage the rest of his life. Nearly thirty years later, at an 1859 treaty council in Blue Earth County, Decora would demand Ho-Chunk pensions, equal to those that white veterans of the Black Hawk War had received.[3]

In 1832, US officials coerced Ho-Chunk leaders into signing treaties that ceded their eastern lands amid worsened anti-Indian sentiment after the Black Hawk War. This left them

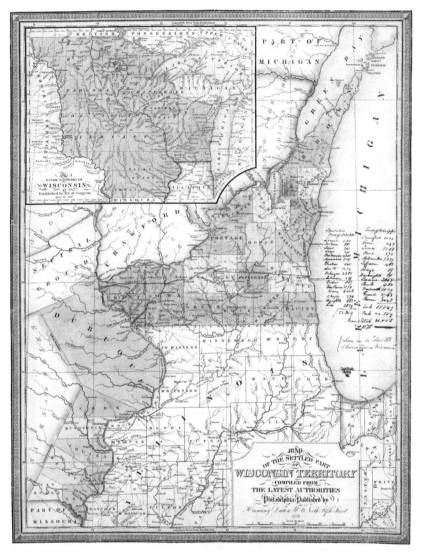

Map of Wisconsin Territory, 1838. *Wisconsin Historical Society,*
WHI-108049

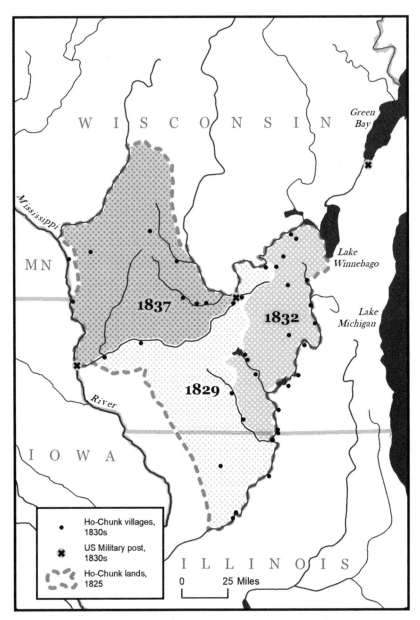

Ho-Chunk lands as defined in the Treaty of Prairie du Chien, 1825, showing subsequent cessions. *Map by Cole Sutton*

with the area between the Black and Mississippi Rivers and contained a mandate for the Ho-Chunk to move to a reservation in northeastern Iowa known as the Neutral Ground, which included a small slice of what would become Minnesota. There they were to act as a buffer between Sauk and Meskwaki (Sac and Fox) and Dakota people. As more settler-colonists arrived in the region, Michigan prepared for statehood and Wisconsin Territory encompassed what was still the Ho-Chunk Nation's sovereign land in 1836. In yet another blow to the Ho-Chunk Nation, a smallpox epidemic in 1834 killed about a quarter of the Ho-Chunk population, reducing their numbers by fifteen hundred.[4]

Expulsion to the Neutral Ground

By 1837, the clamor for removal of all Ho-Chunk people from Wisconsin had reached a fever pitch as settler-colonists began to anticipate the formation of their own state. Barely recovered from the devastation of the epidemic, Ho-Chunk leaders traveled to Washington to "negotiate" a treaty that paved the way for Wisconsin statehood and formally forced the Ho-Chunk Nation to cede the remainder of their homeland. This treaty demanded that all Ho-Chunk people immediately move to the Iowa reservation. However, many Ho-Chunk did not recognize this treaty because the treaty signers were not members of the Bear clan and thus not leaders authorized to negotiate land cessions. Many groups refused to leave. Ho-Chunk leaders later recounted that they were threatened with death if they did not sign this treaty.[5]

US officials sent soldiers to remove them in 1840, and the Ho-Chunk protested at every camp. People sobbed, kissed the ground, and lamented the forced abandonment of their ancestors'—and their recently deceased relatives'—resting places. A group of elderly women on the Kickapoo River begged the soldiers to kill them rather than force them to leave their homes on an impossible journey. The soldiers permitted the women to remain, along with three young men to hunt for them. However, they brought most Ho-Chunk people to Prairie du Chien for transportation to Iowa.[6]

Ho-Chunk people were so attached to their homeland that the government's forced removal efforts were unsuccessful. From this point on, the Ho-Chunk Nation consistently expressed to the federal government a desire to remain on or return to their Wisconsin homeland, and over the years, many left distant reservations to go home. Constant complaints by Wisconsin settler-colonists brought several attempts to round up Ho-Chunk people yet again for forced relocation. At times, the government even offered payments for their detainment, which they then deducted from Ho-Chunk tribal annuities. But with federal and state governments unwilling to fully fund an intensive forced relocation effort, and with bounty hunters incapable of the task, many Ho-Chunk people were able to sidestep removal from Wisconsin. Furthermore, some returned when they faced desperate conditions on the reservations established for them. There were about four hundred Ho-Chunks estimated in Wisconsin after the 1840 removal effort, a number that increased to around one thousand by 1871.[7]

One particularly dissident Ho-Chunk leader refused to leave and told US officials of his great love for his Wisconsin homeland his entire life. Wakanjaxeriga (Roaring Thunder) was known as Dandy by the settler-colonists because of his colorful and elaborate dress. When Governor Henry Dodge had him arrested and imprisoned for refusing to leave Wisconsin in 1844, Wakanjaxeriga demanded an audience with the governor. He asked Dodge if he thought the Bible was a good book and if following that book was all that was required of any man. When Dodge answered affirmatively,

Wakanjaxeriga (Roaring Thunder), known by whites as Dandy, about 1866. *Photo by James F. Bodtker, Wisconsin Historical Society, WHI-61426*

Wakanjaxeriga told him to "look that book all through, and if you find in it that Dandy ought to be removed by the government to Turkey River, then I will go right off." This incarceration left his feet and legs blistered, and he was unable to walk for weeks. Soldiers finally carried him to a carriage to bring him to the reservation, but by this time he had been feigning his injuries, and he easily escaped his captors during the journey. He would never be moved from his cherished home and died there in 1870.[8]

During the early decades of official exile, Ho-Chunk people used different strategies to remain in Wisconsin. Leaders like Yellow Thunder, who had also been arrested for removal and escaped, purchased tracts of land and gained legal title to their homes. Others, like Wakanjaxeriga, withdrew into the woods and moved often. All adapted their lives to the new reality of their homeland. Aside from minimal business interactions, they avoided whites and relied on traditional lifeways. Their distance from settler-colonists in Wisconsin during these years helped them to hold on to their culture.[9]

Meanwhile, a contingent of Ho-Chunk people spent a decade at the Neutral Ground reservation in what is now Iowa, but they did not always remain on the reservation as the nearby settler-colonists wanted. They left the reservation to hunt or do business in the area and of course often returned to Wisconsin. The mere presence of Indigenous people made nearby whites uneasy, so—like the settler-colonists in Wisconsin—they regularly advocated to government officials that the Ho-Chunk be moved. When Ho-Chunk leaders were told that the new reservation would be west of the Mississippi River, they chose land in southwestern Minnesota. But they ended up with a reservation in central Minnesota on a landscape that was unfamiliar to them and incompatible with their lifestyle. And that would not be the end of the moving.[10]

4 HO-CHUNK REMOVALS IN MINNESOTA TERRITORY

When Ho-Chunk people first arrived in the state, Minnesotans hailed the news. After an 1847 economic downturn, settler-colonists welcomed a new Ho-Chunk reservation that brought much-needed business activity to the state from tribal annuities received as payment for their land and spent at nearby businesses. Even better, annuities included payments in hard currency—gold and silver—which was desperately scarce and essential for payments of debts among settler-colonists. While Wisconsin settler-colonists were anxious to get rid of Ho-Chunk people, some Minnesota businessmen lobbied to bring tribal nations and their treaty payments into the state. As the government looked for a tract of land, Ho-Chunk leaders asked for land in Wisconsin; their second choice was the Mankato region. They also eyed land on the Missouri River near Omaha.[1]

The Ho-Chunk sought help in identifying a new reservation from Henry Mower Rice, a former fur trader who had been their agent in Iowa. Rice became a politician and businessman, well-known in Minnesota history for his rivalry with Henry Sibley and for his involvement with questionable business and treaty dealings in which he always profited. Examples of this are the government contracts he received during the Ho-Chunk removal to Long Prairie. He had gained influence as a fur trader with the Ho-Chunk and Ojibwe because of his ability to speak several languages and to navigate intercultural intricacies, including Indigenous gift systems. He represented Ho-Chunk people at the treaty of Fond du Lac, and he included Ho-Chunk contractors with his own bids to the government. But just a few years after they arrived in Minnesota, Rice had begun to lose influence with the Ho-Chunk because he betrayed their trust in his rise to power and wealth.[2]

Long Prairie, an Unsuitable Land

Rice selected a tract of land near Long Prairie in present-day central Minnesota to serve as a new reservation, and the US government purchased it from the Ojibwe in 1847. And although Rice had promised the government he would convince the Ho-Chunk to go willingly, the government again used soldiers to force the Ho-Chunk on a long trek to central Minnesota. Ho-Chunk leaders had requested land in southern Minnesota, but the land Rice selected was more favorable to his pocketbook. He isolated the Ho-Chunk from other traders in order to monopolize their business when annuity payments were made.[3]

Historian Martin Case has described treaty making with tribal nations in the United States as "a network of business interests," and treaty signers in Minnesota demonstrated exactly this idea. Rice—much like his counterpart trader to the Dakota, Henry Sibley—rose to the top of this system in Minnesota, in part thanks to his role as trader to the Ho-Chunk. The treaty system locked tribal nations into cycles of debt to the traders, who often received exclusive access to treaty payments. These traders issued credit to tribes struggling with forced assimilation while being confined to

Henry Mower Rice, about 1860. *Engraving from E. D. Neill,* History of Minnesota, *Minnesota Historical Society*

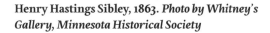

Henry Hastings Sibley, 1863. *Photo by Whitney's Gallery, Minnesota Historical Society*

reservations that could not support their subsistence patterns. Treaty payments were sometimes given directly to the traders to pay off debts, leaving tribal leaders with no choice but to again ask for credit. Traders like Rice found even more clever ways to squeeze personal profit from the reservation system.[4]

The Long Prairie reservation was problematic for the Ho-Chunk from the start. First, Minnesota officials chose this area intentionally to function as a buffer zone between the feuding Dakota and Ojibwe peoples. Next, the landscape was covered with more forest than prairie grass, as the Ho-Chunk were accustomed to and requested. The Ho-Chunk people complained of mosquitoes, unsuitable farmland, and most devastatingly, the lack of sufficient game. The Long Prairie reservation was also too far from their Wisconsin home and relatives, not to mention inaccessible to other trade markets. Henry Rice and those who worked for him had virtually no competition in Long Prairie and were able to push their profits at the expense of the Ho-Chunk.[5]

Despite the distance, many Ho-Chunk families returned to their Wisconsin homelands. Others never left Iowa. In exchange for supporting Zachary Taylor's Whig candidate for territorial delegate, Rice, a Democrat, was awarded a contract to "remove" all these Ho-Chunk families to the reservation, at a fabulous sum of $70 per person. Territorial Governor Alexander Ramsey and Territorial Representative Henry Sibley wrote to Commissioner of Indian Affairs Orlando Brown in the spring of 1850 in an attempt to block the contract. Sibley reasoned that the government was wasting its money because removal was both an impossible and a futile task. He told Brown that the Ho-Chunk were opposed to remaining on the reservation and "will, after the receipt of their annuities, again return to their old haunts in [Wisconsin]." Sibley further argued that Rice had lost influence with the Ho-Chunk and was greatly exaggerating the number of people living off the reservation.

Alexander Ramsey, about 1848. *Minnesota Historical Society*

He reminded Brown that the army had been necessary to force them to move the last time Rice was given the contract. Meanwhile, Ramsey outright requested the commissioner skip any bounties or diplomacy attempts and immediately use the army. Brown replied that a forced removal by the army might cause bloodshed, or the Ho-Chunk would just further scatter, making it more difficult to find them. In the end, Rice was paid for hundreds of Ho-Chunk people he claimed to have brought to the Long Prairie reservation.[6]

Ho-Chunk leaders began working toward a more suitable environment almost immediately. Since the Ho-Chunk were very unhappy, and nearby settler-colonists complained as well, Territorial Governors Alexander Ramsey and Willis Gorman considered new locations for the next reservation. Ramsey first opposed the Ho-Chunk requests for a new reservation before agreeing to support a land exchange. Long Prairie area businessmen like Rice resisted a relocation and were able to get the support of both the Ho-Chunk's agent and the commissioner of Indian Affairs before Gorman replaced Ramsey in 1853. Unlike most officials, Governor Gorman seemed determined to find a home that would satisfy the Ho-Chunk and maintain the promise made by the government. Unfortunately, every site proposed met with strong opposition.[7]

Willis Gorman, about 1860.
Minnesota Historical Society

More Negotiations and Another Move

In 1853, the Ho-Chunk signed a treaty that created a reservation in the Minnetonka area, near the Mississippi River and closer to their preferred location farther south, near where the Blue Earth River joins the Minnesota River at the great bend in the Minnesota River. Settler-colonists around the state as well as the Minnesota territorial press expressed opposition to a treaty that would evict whites to create another reservation. Whites had taken the area from the Dakota people only recently, in 1851. The Ho-Chunk's agent also opposed this reservation, citing their experience with "vicious whites." Congress returned an amended version of the treaty that offered a choice of three different locations previously requested by tribal leaders, but the Ho-Chunk rejected it. The record shows contradictions in Ho-Chunk approval of this treaty, which is probably evidence of tribal divisions and of the tendency for government officials to recognize whomever they saw fit as Ho-Chunk leaders to sign treaties.[8]

It took two more years to negotiate and secure a new treaty, and by then the lumber on the Long Prairie reservation had become more valuable than the business created by its annuities. Henry Rice, now engaged in the timber business, was again involved with administration and implementation of the move, even though he had proven to act only in his own economic interests. But the Ho-Chunk leaders had selected the land for their reservation this time, and it was the same choice

The Mankato Union Office at 230 South Front Street, Mankato, 1862.
Blue Earth County Historical Society

some leaders had made back in 1846 before they were moved to the despised Long Prairie reservation. This land in Blue Earth County was about ten miles south of the new settlement of Mankato, established in 1852; its name is considered a misspelling of Mahkato, the Dakota word for Blue Earth.

So the Ho-Chunk agreed to exchange their central Minnesota land for a smaller reservation in Blue Earth County in 1855. This of course brought Ho-Chunk people on to recently ceded Dakota lands in the tension-filled years before the US–Dakota War of 1862.[9]

5 THE THEFT OF MINNESOTA AND THE CALL FOR EXTERMINATION

The land that is now Minnesota was first the homeland of the Dakota, then later of the Ojibwe and Ho-Chunk peoples. Origin stories of the Dakota, part of the Oceti Sakowiŋ (Seven Council Fires, also called the Sioux) state that they have always been in Mni Sota Makoce, the land where the water reflects the sky. Before Europeans arrived, Ojibwe groups had moved into the area from the east and north—the Great Lakes region. Eastern bands of Dakota inhabited southern Minnesota in the early nineteenth century, with the Mdewakanton Dakota occupying Bdote, the confluence of the Mississippi and Minnesota Rivers. They first traded for European goods with other tribal nations in the seventeenth century; in subsequent centuries, they traded with a succession of explorers and then French, British, and American fur traders. When Ho-Chunk leaders were signing their first land cession treaties with Americans who had already moved on to their mines in the 1830s and 1840s, the Mdewakanton Dakota leader Little Crow and other Dakota leaders were also traveling to Washington to lay diplomatic foundations. They, too, watched as Americans set up permanent settlements that were far more intrusive than those built by the French and British during the fur-trade era.[1]

Government negotiators and traders forced the Wahpeton, Sisseton, Mdewakanton, and Wahpekute bands of Dakota to sign the 1851 Treaties of Traverse des Sioux and Mendota, which together opened most of southern Minnesota to settler-colonists. In exchange for promises of annual treaty payments and a lump sum that was mostly taken by traders claiming inflated debts, the Dakota people surrendered almost thirty-five million acres of land and moved to reservations that were too small to accommodate their lifestyle, culture, or even basic subsistence. Missionaries and government agents encouraged the Dakota to farm in order to adapt to the new, smaller hunting grounds. The government agents who doled out payments even showed favoritism to the farmer Indians as an incentive for giving up traditional lifeways. They provided food and equipment to Dakota who took up farming—and denied them to those who did not. However, most Dakota people continued to depend on hunting and annuities for subsistence. As whites rushed to establish preemption claims on the land surrounding the reservation, game became even more scarce. Some Dakota families turned to subsistence farming that often suffered from bad crop years, especially droughts. A late annuity payment from the government increasingly meant great hardship or death.[2]

At this point, the Ho-Chunk and Dakota peoples had different priorities. The Ho-Chunk moved near the southwestern Minnesota Dakota reservation in 1855, just when conditions were becoming unbearable for the Dakota. The Dakota were experiencing frustration over a decade of white encroachment that robbed them of their resources and threatened their culture. Like the Ho-Chunk in the decades prior, the Dakota deeply resented the treaties and the settler-colonists, who constantly trespassed on Dakota reservation lands. But by now, many Ho-Chunk leaders seemed to want an acceptable permanent home after removals from two unsatisfactory reservations. Even though, once again, they had first appealed to have a reservation in Wisconsin, the Ho-Chunk who moved to Blue Earth County believed, and the government promised, that it would be their last move. Unlike the previous two reservations, this prime farmland, selected by the Ho-Chunk themselves, was an acceptable location to make their home.[3]

Unfortunately, there were pressures building just north of their new home that the Ho-Chunk knew all too well. During the 1850s, whites in Blue Earth County, as well as settler-colonists in other areas under consideration, like Montevideo and Minnetonka, organized mass protests when they heard news of the planned reservation.

Settler-colonists turned out en masse to object when the government signed a treaty with the Ho-Chunk in 1855. This treaty evicted all preemptors living in six townships in Blue Earth County and two in neighboring Steele (later Waseca) County, plus parts of the townships to the north of this block; it provided the preemptors with compensation in order to make way for a Ho-Chunk reservation. When their agent employed the county surveyor to draw the boundary lines in April, nineteenth-century Blue Earth County historian Thomas Hughes noted that "all there was left of our once magnificent fine county was a thin shell embracing at its center a big Indian reservation." So on June 2, 1855, settler-colonists within or near the reservation lines held an opposition meeting with a chairperson, secretary, and orators, raising "the most vigorous protests against these confiscations of their territory."[4]

This assembly signed resolutions expressing a concern for the safety of nearby settler-colonists, but mostly they complained about losing land that they did not even own. Their preemption claims were based on an 1854 law that allowed people to file an intention to purchase public lands that they improved and occupied. Despite the settler-colonists' objections to "the [government] putting so many savages as a menace

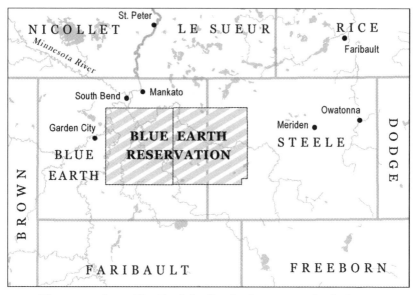

The reservation at Blue Earth in 1855. In 1857 western Steele County became Waseca County; other surrounding counties were also redefined. *Map by Cole Sutton*

The aptly named Basil Moreland, about 1858. He was elected to Minnesota's first state legislature in 1857 as a senator from Mankato. *Photo by Hill, Kelley & Company, Minnesota Historical Society*

to the lives and property of the adjacent white settlements," almost two thousand Ho-Chunk people arrived in mid-June of 1855. Some settler-colonists refused to give up their claims to the Ho-Chunk land. Basil Moreland built a homestead on the Blue Earth River in 1854, the year he served as Blue Earth County sheriff. He lived alongside the Ho-Chunk for several years before being evicted—then moving back, then again leaving. He continued this issue in court for most of his life, finally reaching a settlement with the government fifty years after filing his first claim. Other settler-colonists moved off the reservation but continued for years to make claims to the government.[5]

Taking More

Minnesotans, reeling from economic troubles brought on by the panic of 1857, reached statehood in 1858, the year Mankato received its charter as a city. The state's citizens set their sights on obtaining even more Indigenous lands. Dakota diplomats traveled to Washington in 1858 in order to request enforcement of existing treaties and stop settler-colonists from taking land on the reservation. But government officials detained them and forced them to sign a devastating new treaty. This treaty cut their reservation in half and allotted the remaining half to individual families. The Dakota people were both heartbroken and furious at the news that they must give more land to their antagonists and divide the property they had always held in common.

Immediately after obtaining this land from the Dakota, the government turned to the Ho-Chunk reservation with the same purpose in mind. In 1859, as the annuities paid under earlier treaties were expiring, the government pressed Ho-Chunk leaders to sell half their recently acquired Blue Earth County reservation and parcel the remainder into eighty-acre

allotments. After a year's time, during which Ho-Chunk families living elsewhere could move to Blue Earth and receive allotments, the unassigned lands would be sold to white farmers.
Winneshiek adamantly opposed the treaty put before him, so
the government agents unseated him. Other leaders tried to
negotiate the best deal possible. Waukon Decora reminded the
treaty council of federal obligations to the Ho-Chunk people
for their service in the Black Hawk War and other conflicts.
Baptiste LaSallier, another leader, requested debts due under
other treaties. He told the treaty council that if they expected
Ho-Chunk people to act like white men, "We want to tell
you that it takes a great deal of money to do so." The government promised once again to pay its debts to the Ho-Chunk

**Baptiste LaSallier,
Ho-Chunk leader,
about 1855.** *Minnesota
Historical Society*

OPPOSITE. The reser-
vation at Blue Earth,
1855 to 1863, showing
the lands purchased
by members of the
Knights of the Forest,
with dates of purchase.
Map by Cole Sutton

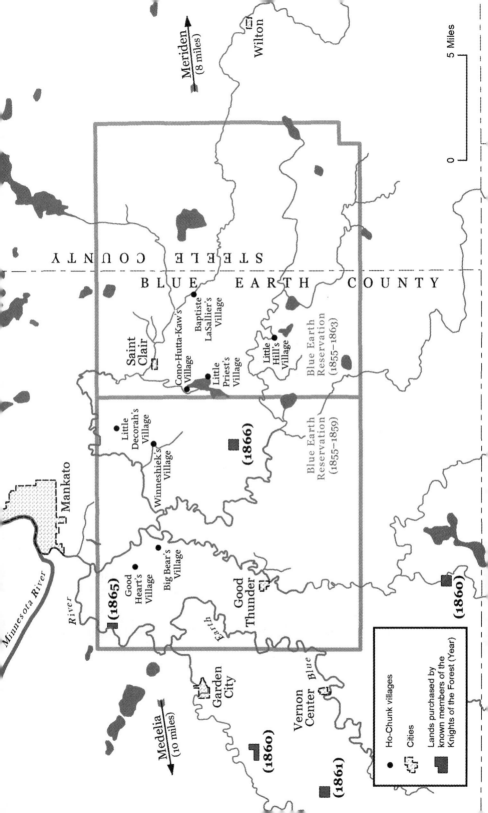

and continued the treaty negotiations without Winneshiek. Government representatives then decided they recognized LaSallier as the head chief and awarded him a medal for "rendering himself obnoxious to the wrath of the rebel Winneshiek." But Winneshiek still had influence as a leader among his people, and Americans had no authority to overthrow him.[6]

Historian Thomas Hughes, who recorded the history of Mankato and Blue Earth County in the nineteenth century. *Minnesota Historical Society*

Historian Thomas Hughes describes an ominous incident in January 1859 in the nearby town of Danville: "There were numerous scraps and misunderstandings which served to keep the neighborhood from stagnation. The two main causes of friction were claim jumping and selling liquor to Indians. About 1859 one John Burns was shot at and slightly wounded by a Winnebago Indian, whom it is claimed he had filled with too much fire water. The Indian was taken to Mankato and boarded and lodged a few weeks at the county's expense and then was permitted to escape."

Nonetheless, this incident had "stirred up the military spirit of the county" three years before the war. According to Hughes, "There was much activity among the militia companies in the county," and "During the winter [of 1859–60] large public meetings were held . . . to agitate the matter" of moving the Ho-Chunk people.[7]

Ho-Chunks were determined to hold on to their reservation and their collective identity. The 1859 treaty stripped them of half their Blue Earth County reservation. Although it was not ratified until 1861, whites began moving on to the land. Winneshiek then attempted to prevent implementation of treaty stipulations that carved the remainder of their land into individual allotments. This requirement threatened the Ho-Chunk way of life and sovereignty by taking away their traditional shared land ownership in favor of individual ownership. Winneshiek and his men broke the surveyor's instruments and attempted to block his entrance to parts of their

Coming Thunder Winneshiek, probably photographed in May 1863 at the Fort Snelling camp. *Photo by Benjamin F. Upton, Minnesota Historical Society*

land. Protesters then proceeded among those in an enroll-
ment line, "vociferating at the top of their voices," convincing
most people to refuse the roll call. Winneshiek had evidently
"made up his mind deliberately to defy the government." The
surveyor requested the government imprison Winneshiek,
so Superintendent Clark Thompson sent for troops from Fort
Ridgley to make the arrest. Meanwhile, the agent withheld
the distribution of goods to anyone who declined to enroll for
land allotments. In the end, they did not need soldiers to calm
Winneshiek's efforts. The surveyor used old lists to create the
allotment list.[8]

This treaty dramatically cut the Ho-Chunk land base
and relegated the people to allotted farmland. This pattern
of ownership further eroded their traditional communal
lifestyle. Their agent expressed Ho-Chunks' concern for the
permanence of their home and pointed out their reluctance
to erect buildings or plow fields until they knew for certain
they would remain at this reservation. After so many false
starts, some Ho-Chunk people disagreed with Winneshiek
and believed the allotments might give them an enduring
legal title to their property, thus guaranteeing that they could
stay on it. Until they held legal title to their allotments, many
were hesitant to make serious improvements to their land. In
the meantime, they made money from digging ginseng and
selling it to Mankato businessmen.[9]

Opposition, Agitation, Objections, Petitions

Settler-colonists and county leaders agitated for Ho-Chunk
removal throughout their entire tenure in the county, begin-
ning with the 1855 objection to the reservation's creation.
Because settler-colonists had already preempted homesteads
on the land and the county leaders thought their political
boundaries had been set, they took it as a hard and personal

economic loss when the territorial legislature ejected settler-colonists in favor of a reservation. The practice of preemption was a standard method of land acquisition during American colonization, but it did not always result in legal ownership of the land. Historian Thomas Hughes describes the arrival of Ho-Chunk people with a chapter titled, unironically, "Loss of Territory," noting, "the exceptional bright prospects of our county were doomed to a sudden and unexpected eclipse." Leaders and settler-colonists in Blue Earth County continued to protest the presence of Ho-Chunk people in the area throughout their tenancy. Lawmakers and citizens passed several resolutions and petitions over the years at many different levels to promote the elimination of the reservation.[10]

Politics, progress, and profiteering were all factors in the call for removal, but ethnic culture clashes were a pervasive force as well. The arrival of the Ho-Chunk people in central Minnesota had been lauded as an economic boon back in 1847, but by 1855 settler-colonists in southwestern Minnesota viewed Native reservations as obstacles to the area's advancement. Historian Bruce White has documented the social shift in Minnesota during this period. As Indigenous people were forced onto reservations during the territorial years, Minnesota transformed from a multiethnic world of fur traders and cultural brokers of mixed ancestry to one ruled by an American market mentality. Traders who remained transformed their work to the "Indian trade," supplying treaty goods purchased cheaply and making other trades that took as much money as possible from Native people who received payments for the land. Much like the Wisconsin settler-colonists before them, and like others pouring across the continent, Minnesotans believed they would make better use of the land than Ho-Chunk people would. Hughes recounted the settler-colonists' dismay that the reservation encompassed the "very best farmlands in the county." But they also worried that the presence of the reservation might impede the area's growth by slowing white immigration.[11]

In his *History of Blue Earth County*, Hughes relates one story of white immigrants on their way to the county who met a large group of Ho-Chunk immigrants on their way to the new reservation there. Hughes wrote that "The sight of so many savages and the thought that they were to be such close neighbors, rather intimidated our immigrants and they halted some days in doubt whether to advance, retreat or go elsewhere." These travelers evidently decided to continue their move to Blue Earth County, but anecdotes and attitudes like this worried area leaders: Minnesota's growth might bypass their county as long as the reservation was there. Mankato and Blue Earth County histories that appeared in marketing and historical publications in the late nineteenth century nearly all describe the years of the reservation's existence as a pause in the county's early development.[12]

Race and culture clashes were the main feature in removal rhetoric from the start, and although there were instances of friendship between settler-colonists and Ho-Chunk people, most encounters in the county only served to confirm biases and fears in the minds of whites. Hughes describes one 1855 "Indian scare" near the reservation when a group of white men determined to chase down a report of possible attacks after gunshots were heard, only to find a single Ho-Chunk teenager. Apparently, the boy "was quite friendly with the settlers and a favorite among them . . . and he burst into a big laugh, and explained how he had been out hunting with other Indians on Rice Lake." In another 1855 incident, Mankatoans were upset that Ho-Chunk people had "painted the village red," so they "turned out en masse and broke up all the liquor shops in town and poured the liquors into the streets." The stores had sold alcohol to the Ho-Chunks, against a local law that banned the sale of intoxicants to Native people.[13]

But even when there was no alcohol or hunting involved,

white residents expressed irrational fears of their Ho-Chunk neighbors. The Mankato newspapers repeatedly referred to the Ho-Chunk people in Blue Earth County as "savages" and "annoyances," whose differences were feared. According to Hughes, most settler-colonists near the reservation acquired "a good savage watch dog" because they often received neighborly requests for food or assistance from Ho-Chunk people. The reciprocal exchange of food and gifts was an important part of culture and alliance-building for all Indigenous nations in Minnesota Territory, but white settler-colonists perceived these visits as Ho-Chunk people begging for food. In fact, Indigenous people lived a very different cultural etiquette around visiting, sharing food, and property.[14]

In February 1858, just a few months before statehood, Minnesota's territorial legislature sent a joint resolution to the US Congress to promote the removal of the Ho-Chunk people from the state (see Appendix A). The resolution complained that Ho-Chunk people were "constantly being supplied with spirituous liquors" by local whites and "the civilization of these Indians would doubtless be greatly advanced by removing them beyond the influence above alluded to." The irony of this statement was apparently lost on legislators. However, the real purpose of the resolution was economics. The document sent to Congress aimed to stop business relationships between whites and Ho-Chunk people altogether, stating that it was "impossible to prevent a constant trade being carried on between the white settlers and the Indians occupying the said reserve." Minnesota legislators implied to the federal government that they, too, had a financial stake in removing Ho-Chunk people from the state because "lands sold by the United States are not taxable until patents therefor have been issued."[15]

While the national Democrats and Republicans fought over slavery and other Civil War issues in 1862, the Blue Earth County partisans engaged in a fierce argument over which party was more anti-Indian. The two Mankato newspapers, which represented opposing political parties, accused each other as well as politicians from the opposite party of not working hard enough or taking the right steps toward the removal effort. The competition between the parties to be most active for Ho-Chunk removal meant the overall effort was bipartisan. As the settler-colonists, agents, and traders along with crop failures put increasing pressure on the living conditions of Indigenous people in Minnesota and government payments for their land were perpetually late, both the Dakota and the Ho-Chunk became more desperate.[16]

Warfare, Terror, and Calls for Extermination

After a bad crop year combined with another late annuity payment, the Dakota were left near starvation in the summer of 1862. Their traders dealt another blow by cutting off credit. Dakota people began to demand that traders open their food warehouses to alleviate hunger. The situation escalated when Andrew Myrick told starving Dakota people gathered at his warehouse to "eat grass or their own dung." Many tense encounters at the Lower and Upper Sioux Agencies came close to bloodshed before violence erupted on August 18. The annuity payment for the Dakota arrived in Minnesota too late, as tensions reached the breaking point.[17]

When a few young Dakota men murdered a family of settler-colonists near Acton, Dakota soldiers decided the time was right for war. Some Dakota leaders refused to engage in the war. But after trying unsuccessfully to dissuade the young soldiers, Mdewakanton chief Little Crow reluctantly agreed to lead the men into what he expected to be their deaths. They then sent a contingent to request assistance from the Ho-Chunk. Although several Ho-Chunk men left the Blue Earth reservation to fight with the Dakota, there was no general move to join the war. Their agent, Saint Andre Durand

Balcombe, reported that because of their refusal to join, the Ho-Chunk "lived in fear of an attack from the Sioux, and have almost daily implored me for protection." Alexander Ramsey sent two companies of soldiers at the agent's request, purportedly to assure the Ho-Chunk's safety. But it also pacified the nearby whites, whose "idle threats . . . frightened the Winnebago some."[18]

The Dakota warring forces first attacked the agencies and raided the countryside before confronting New Ulm. Several battles followed at Fort Ridgley, Birch Coulee, and Wood Lake, where the Dakota fighters eventually lost their initial gains and fled toward Canada. Other Dakota who had not joined the fighting surrendered to their long-trusted trader and agent, Henry Sibley, who broke all promises of immunity by tricking the men into surrendering their weapons, separating them from the elders, women, and children, and putting them on trial. The military tribunal he convened, against military law, sentenced 302 Dakota men to death during unfair trials that were as brief as five minutes. Sibley's forces then escorted the men to Mankato to await President Abraham Lincoln's review of the execution orders. Lincoln eventually approved the execution of thirty-eight men found guilty of attacking civilians rather than battle participants.

Saint Andre Durand Balcombe, a member of Minnesota's territorial legislature, about 1858. He was agent to the Ho-Chunk from 1861 to 1865. *Minnesota Historical Society*

The intense anti-Indian fervor and its implications for the Ho-Chunk and all tribal nations in the region were evident immediately following the first bloodshed. Governor Alexander Ramsey declared on September 9 that "The Sioux Indians of Minnesota must be exterminated or driven forever beyond the borders of the State." Newspapers in Mankato, St. Paul, and St. Cloud called for removal, retribution, and even extermination. Minnesotans believed all Native people to be guilty, and that included Dakota women, children, and elderly, as well as men who had not participated in the war. It was not long before the removal rhetoric also included nearby Indigenous nations who did not share a common identity with the Dakota. Even the Ojibwe in the Minnesota north woods, far from larger white settlements, felt the consequences of the US–Dakota War. The panic reached as far as Wisconsin, with people there once again frantically attempting to have the remaining Ho-Chunk people removed. Settler-colonists repeatedly argued that the US–Dakota War was proof that white people and Indians could not coexist in peace.[19]

In early November, as General Henry Sibley was moving the imprisoned men to Mankato to await execution, settler-colonists warned him of a possible attack on his Dakota prisoners of war. As they approached New Ulm, the city's residents were engaged in digging new graves for loved ones hastily buried during the battles. Sibley led the condemned Dakota around the town to avoid a clash, but an enraged mob of mostly women attacked them with stones, hatchets, and boiling water. Civic leaders of New Ulm and Brown County partially planned—or at the very least, encouraged—the attack on the Dakota prisoners outside of New Ulm. Sibley failed to serve justice to the instigators, but he did manage to prevent an unreserved massacre that day.

Minnesotans soon showed they were prepared to attack any Native person they saw, not just the combatants proclaimed guilty by a military tribunal. Sibley wanted to ensure that law and order prevailed in the treatment of the Dakota people, rather than mob attacks. He charged Colonel William Marshall with ensuring the safety of the procession of women, children, and elderly Dakota as they traveled to Fort Snelling, where they were to be confined. White people in Henderson brutally confronted Dakota people near the city, where one woman threw a nursing Dakota baby to the ground; hours later, the child died. Marshall faced the same difficulties as Sibley, in that his soldiers were not necessarily willing to protect the Dakota. It was clear that even the women, babies, and elderly were under threat of death.[20]

Once the Dakota people had arrived at their respective destinations for the winter, some Minnesotans worried that President Lincoln would set them all free. Some settler-colonists became determined that no Dakota people would make it out of the state alive. Dakota family members were vulnerable to

Colonel William Marshall, about 1864. *Photo by Whitney's Gallery, Minnesota Historical Society*

nearby whites even while under military guard in the Fort Snelling internment camp over the winter. Minnesotans seethed with the desire for vengeance. The internment of Dakota women, children, and elders only made some settler-colonists angrier, because they were alive. Rumors that the Dakota prisoners would not be executed spread throughout the region, and Minnesota men began to travel to Mankato to ensure the Dakota men were killed. They did not wait for the federal government to make a decision that might be lenient.[21]

For the few weeks between Sibley's departure from Mankato on November 25 and Lincoln's decision to execute thirty-eight Dakota in late December, Colonel Stephen Miller, whom Sibley left in charge of the Mankato camp, attempted to control growing public hostility against the prisoners. On December 4, 1862, in a dramatic showdown on the Blue Earth bridge in Mankato, Miller put his own life and money on the line to stop an advancing mob on its way to kill the prisoners. He called troops from the Ho-Chunk agency into Mankato to help arrest the ringleaders of about 150 to 200 armed agitators, many who had come down from St. Peter and possibly New Ulm; the leaders were eventually released. Miller then moved the prisoners to a more secure location in the center of town. He also dispatched German spies to infiltrate "an extensive secret organization including men of character in all this upper country, including soldiers," who had plans to murder the prisoners. Miller personally selected and paid his own spies to infiltrate these organizations in an attempt to stay one step ahead of the organized mob coming his way.[22]

After the confrontation on the bridge, Miller received conflicting reports of the sentiments of Mankato residents toward direct violence against the prisoners. He then approached the Mankato men with an attempt to strong-arm their support in keeping order in the city. He met with leading citizens of

Colonel Stephen
Miller, about 1863.
*Photo by Whitney's
Gallery, Minnesota
Historical Society*

Mankato at least twice, seeking to gain their assistance in the
protection of Dakota prisoners and threatening the entire city
with military force if citizens did not remain peaceful. At the
first meeting, late in November, the Mankato men expressed
their concern that the prisoners might leave the city alive.
Miller attempted to calm the city leaders and enlist their help
by reminding them of their civic duty. However, reports that
Blue Earth county sheriff Daniel Tyner was instigating public anger showed Miller that local officials were not interested
in enforcing the law when it came to the Dakota prisoners.
Miller held a second meeting with Mankato leaders a few days
after the intense bridge confrontation, where he threatened to

raze the town with cannons if the citizens attacked the prisoners again.[23]

Minnesota governor Alexander Ramsey struggled to deesca-
late the situation. He issued a *Proclamation to the People of Minnesota* on December 6, 1862, likely directed at the mob of men
in Mankato. He called upon "all citizens engaged in these dis-
orderly demonstrations, to desist therefrom." The governor
implored Minnesotans to think about "the good name and
reputation of the people of this state." Although he felt there
was "justification of this . . . high-handed method of retalia-
tion," he knew "the civilized world will not so regard it." He
promised the citizens that Lincoln would allow them to hang
the Dakota prisoners lawfully. Ramsey argued that allowing
the military to execute the prisoners, rather than openly defy-
ing law and order with "the blind fury of a mob" and "barba-
rous violence," would "teach these savage men hereafter to
respect the authority" of the government of Minnesota. He
assured the settler-colonists that Lincoln's decision would
come soon, and if the president decided against execution,
state lawmakers would do so under local laws. They had only
to wait a few more weeks.[24]

6 MANKATO MEN AND THE SECRET SOCIETY TRADITION

On December 26, 1862, the US government executed thirty-eight men in Mankato in the largest mass hanging in US history. An estimated four thousand people packed into Mankato—a town of about fifteen hundred in 1860—to witness the public event. Clergy attended the men as they awaited their fate, attempting last-minute conversions to Christianity. The prisoners sang Dakota songs, including a Presbyterian hymn, as soldiers led them to the scaffolding at 10 AM. They held hands as the drum beat to signal the rope cut. Witnesses describe a moment of silence before the crowd cheered. They were left hanging for a half hour until their bodies were cut down and buried in a mass grave. That night, doctors in the area—including William Worrall Mayo, founder of what became the Mayo Clinic in Rochester—exhumed the bodies for medical study.[1]

The execution in Mankato on December 26, along with the planned expulsion of the Dakota, may have been enough to satisfy citizens of New Ulm and settler-colonists of Brown County, but people in Mankato and Blue Earth County still had the Ho-Chunk reservation in their midst. Settler-colonists wanted the Ho-Chunk people to leave, and they did not care where they went, how they got there, or what

The execution of thirty-eight Dakota men, December 26, 1862, in Mankato. *Pastel drawing by J. Thullen, 1884, Minnesota Historical Society*

happened to them when they arrived. Aggressive public pressure had rid the state of Dakota people; anti–Ho-Chunk residents in Blue Earth County attempted to mimic those tactics for a similar result. The mysterious secret society format of the Knights of the Forest performed that function perfectly. Leaders used racial fearmongering in their initiation rites and oath contained in the pamphlet entitled "Ritual" to create and encourage fear of Ho-Chunk people among rank-and-file Knights members. They condemned all Indigenous people for the war with the Dakota, and so hanging thirty-eight Dakota men would not be enough for Mankato area businessmen.

In later years, newspaper articles revealed the names of three men who belonged to the Knights of the Forest: John F. Meagher, Asa Barney, and Charles A. Chapman. John J. Porter Jr.'s 1929 obituary disclosed his membership. These prominent men left a trail of personal papers, published works, as well as business and government documents. As well-known members of the Knights, they provide solid clues as to the nature of the group as a whole.[2]

CHARLES A. CHAPMAN

When Charles A. Chapman arrived to survey land in Blue Earth County in 1856 at the age of twenty-three, he was a recently graduated, entrepreneurial American man on the make. Born in Cambridge, Massachusetts, in 1833, he grew up the son of Welsh immigrants in New England, which had a thriving and innovative fraternal order scene connected to labor groups, politics, and European revolutionaries. Chapman eventually graduated from Harvard University and moved to Minnesota as a surveyor for a private company. It is more than likely Chapman was familiar with the creation, process, and political function of secret societies before he moved to Minnesota. He was an early member, officer, and historian of the Mankato Masonic Lodge. Thomas Hughes wrote that Chapman's "Harvard training and his cultured New England ancestry" always remained a part of his personality.[3]

Chapman's move to Mankato could not have come at a more opportune time for him. After Minnesota Territory's political leaders had engineered the taking of large swaths of land from the Dakota, the population had grown swiftly,

Charles A. Chapman, Mankato city engineer, Blue Earth County auditor, and member of the Knights of the Forest. *In* Mankato: Its First Fifty Years, *Minnesota Historical Society*

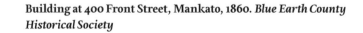

Building at 400 Front Street, Mankato, 1860. *Blue Earth County Historical Society*

and Minnesota was on the verge of gaining statehood. There was plenty of work for surveyors, carving out new towns and homesteads. Furthermore, Mankato was an up-and-coming market town that would soon be at the apex of land sales for the valuable farmlands of southern Minnesota. Chapman promptly set up a surveying business and established himself as a Mankato civic leader and one of the original settler-colonists in South Bend, the settlement across the river from Mankato that rivaled it in the early years. He was involved in surveying much of the county, drawing maps, and laying out new townsites.[4]

Chapman is a major figure in Mankato's earliest history. He was a city engineer, Blue Earth County auditor, and, in 1862, Blue Earth County surveyor. He participated in local government, churches, and other organizations. In short, he became one of the town fathers of Mankato. His 1858 pioneer home is now on the National Register of Historic Places.

The Charles Chapman House, built about 1858 in Mankato. *Photo by Bobak Ha'Eri, 2009, CC-By-SA-3.0*

It is possible Chapman was a leader, or at least a founding member, of the Knights of the Forest, but his outspokenness does not necessarily equate to an administrative role. In 1886 the *Mankato Review* published an unsigned article titled "The Knights of the Forest: A Secret History"; internal evidence suggests Chapman was the author, as some of the text is also used in a 1916 *Daily Review* article that he signed, which was titled "Secret Society of Early Mankato." The 1886 "Secret History" (see Appendix B) is a crucial source. It says that the "Grand Lodge" for the Knights of the Forest was located at Mankato, and there were subordinate "chapters" in nearby towns like Garden City in Blue Earth County and Meriden in Steele County. This suggests the leadership was in Mankato, where Chapman served among the officer ranks of the Mankato masons.[5]

Chapman authored pamphlets, histories, newspaper articles, and business advertisements. He recorded Knights of the Forest history in his *Fifth Annual Report of the Board of Trade of the City of Mankato, Minnesota* in 1878 and in his masonic *History of Mankato Lodge No. 12* in 1902. It is evident from his newspaper articles in later years that he wanted credit for his role in the growth and development of the Mankato area, and he considered his association with the Knights of the Forest to be a significant feature of that legacy. His descriptions of the secret society leave the impression that he might have sometimes presented an embellished version of events in an attempt to secure his legacy as a town father and pioneer hero—but if he did have a leadership role in the Knights of the Forest, he did not claim as much in his reports.

Regardless of whether or not Chapman was a leader, the newspaper articles and several other texts he authored provide the most information to be found about the Knights of the Forest beyond their four-page pamphlet on initiation rites. Although the organization claimed to shroud itself in secrecy, he clearly wanted it to be remembered in history. He wrote several short histories in various publications about the growth and development of the area, and he mentioned the Knights in nearly every one. Though official histories or essays by Chapman simply stated the society existed and its purpose was removal of Ho-Chunk people, he was much more forthcoming in newspaper articles about possible activities of the group. The articles in the *Mankato Review* in the last decades of his life contain much more detail conveyed with obvious pride. They also make explicit the goals of the Knights. Chapman wrote of the Ho-Chunk, "Besides being a constant menace, they were occupying and rendering useless 234 square miles of the best farming land in Blue Earth county." (Chapman's sentiment was clear, but his figures were wrong; the original reservation of 324 square miles was reduced to 162 square miles by 1863.) He was convinced that the prosperity and progress of the county were owed to the long fight for removal of the Ho-Chunk reservation.[6]

Chapman's portrayals of Mankato men, including himself, usually included their ethnicity. He often characterized white settlers such as Jews, Irish, and Welshmen like himself as industrious pioneers paving the way for advancement. However, he described the Ho-Chunk people, who arrived in Blue Earth County in 1855, as "miserable savages" who were "the first great drawback to the prosperity" of the county. He seemed proud of the deadly threat the Knights had posed to the Ho-Chunk people.[7]

Chapman was militantly active for Ho-Chunk removal from Blue Earth County for years before the US-Dakota War. In 1859, he was second sergeant in the Mankato Artillery Company, which had organized in response to the shooting of removal advocate John Burns in January of that year. During this time, a sharpshooters' group also organized at Garden City, which was only a few miles from the Ho-Chunk reservation lines. This militant atmosphere foreshadowed the postwar panic. It appears the US–Dakota War served a useful purpose in pressing a long-standing aggressive demand for Ho-Chunk removal.[8]

THE PORTER FAMILY

John J. Porter Sr. arrived in Blue Earth County with his wife and three sons in 1857 from Lancaster, Pennsylvania. According to Thomas Hughes, Porter immediately invested in and moved to the townsite of Shelbyville just southwest of the Ho-Chunk reservation and constructed a large sawmill there. Porter claimed to be a "personal acquaintance" of President James Buchanan and that the president had promised him the Minnesota Land Office, "which, had it been fulfilled, would have been a big boom for their town site." Like Chapman, he was an entrepreneurial American man on the make when the family moved to Blue Earth County. However, he never received the land office appointment, and the townsite and sawmill were a failure. Porter moved into Mankato just three years later, after Buchanan lost the 1860 election to Abraham Lincoln. Porter opened a tannery, and in 1862 he was elected to the state legislature. When the US–Dakota War commenced, he was still advertising the sale of his farm at the unsuccessful Shelbyville townsite.[9]

Born in 1838, John J. Porter Jr. grew up with his brothers in Pennsylvania during a period of innovation in fraternal orders as political and social organizations in the northeastern United States. Lancaster was the state capitol at the time and a prime example of the kind of city Mankato hoped to become.[10]

John J. Porter Jr. was aged ninety-one when he died in 1929, identified in his obituary as a member of the Knights of the Forest. John J. Porter Sr.'s membership is highly probable, given his public leadership in the removal efforts and his

John J. Porter Sr., Mankato legislator, namesake of Camp Porter, and probable member of the Knights of the Forest, about 1863. No photo has been located of his son, John J. Porter Jr., a member of the Knights of the Forest. *Photo by Moses C. Tuttle, Minnesota Historical Society*

son's acknowledged role. It is not known if the other Porter brothers, Henry and Daniel, belonged to the Knights. Daniel became a war hero, celebrated for his part in the Battle of New Ulm, where he served in the Mankato Home Guards, a militia made up of "citizen soldiers" and headed by John F. Meagher. He continued his military service for several years after 1862, earning a Civil War pension. Henry, born in 1841, registered for the draft in 1863 in Mankato but never started any business ventures or engaged in civic activities in Minnesota. He was the least public of the Porter sons.[11]

E. D. B. Porter, who also arrived from Lancaster, Pennsylvania, around the same time, was likely a relative of the Porter family. He was an officer in the Mankato masons. His signature appears on a petition sent to the commissioner of Indian Affairs in January 1863 calling for the removal of the Ho-Chunk people. E. D. B. belonged to the Frontier Rangers, a militia that patrolled between Mankato, South Bend, and Madelia during the US–Dakota War; it is reasonable to suppose he was also a member of the Knights of the Forest. Interestingly, E. D. B.'s father-in-law was the Ho-Chunk physician, Moses Wickersham, who eventually moved with the Ho-Chunk to Nebraska. After the war, E. D. B. moved to St. Paul and then to the state of Washington, where he worked for the state treasury until he died. Chapman wrote in his history of the Mankato masons that the group convicted E. D. B. of embezzlement after he moved away. E. D. B. denied this via letters from Washington, and he never repaid the stolen money.[12]

John J. Porter Sr. benefited from the Ho-Chunk removal for the rest of his life, both in reputation and financially. During the war, he had traveled to St. Paul, bearing witness of the events in New Ulm, and then assisted the commander while Mankato was under martial law on August 24, 1862. After the war, he won two more elections to the state legislature, where he served until 1865. In 1866, he paid taxes as a real estate agent, an occupation he had not claimed before the removal. He was also involved with reorganizing the Minnesota Valley Railroad and then worked for the St. Paul and Sioux City Railroad Land Office. He died in Mankato, a little more than a decade after the war, and his obituary hailed him as "deservedly popular with the people" for his "active interest in everything pertaining to the welfare of this county and state." The *Mankato Review* memorialized him for "being prominently identified in . . . the removal of the Winnebago Indians." He and his family clearly believed his part in the Ho-Chunk removal to be among his greatest achievements.[13]

Meanwhile, John J. Porter Jr. lived a less consequential life. The only advantage Ho-Chunk removal brought him was his father's successes. He moved to St. Paul sometime after the US–Dakota War. He and his wife most likely relocated in the early 1870s, when his father died and his father-in-law became proprietor of the International Hotel in St. Paul. Porter worked as a clerk there and as a freight inspector. He lived and worked nearly forty years in St. Paul before spending the last nineteen years of his life in the care of his daughter in Illinois. It is fitting that in his obituary, the *Mankato Free Press* remembered him as the "the last surviving member of the Knights of the Forest." His involvement with the group was his foremost legacy to the town.[14]

Politicians like John J. Porter Sr. were responsible for bringing those mysterious threats from secret societies, implied or explicit, to the halls of government. In the end, he was the most public, vigorous agitator for removal in Mankato. It is significant that the location along the river in Mankato where the Ho-Chunk awaited removal in the spring of 1863 was named "Camp Porter." According to Hughes, this was to "honor John J. Porter [Sr.], who had been most active in their removal."[15]

THE BARNEY BROTHERS

Asa Barney was another young settler-colonist from the northeastern United States who moved to Minnesota territory with ambitions like those of Chapman and the Porters. Born in 1835, Barney grew up in New York, and he followed his two older brothers to Mankato in 1857. Charles was first to arrive, following the death of their father in 1855. The eldest brother, Sheldon, moved to Minnesota immediately after his admission to the bar in 1856 and opened a law practice in Mankato. The brothers proclaimed an exclusively American heritage, with Charles Barney's biography stating that they descended both from Benjamin Franklin and from a settler who arrived in Salem, Massachusetts, in 1634. They were probably well versed in the possibilities for political and social power in secret societies.[16]

LEFT: Asa Barney, bookkeeper, businessman, and member of the Knights of the Forest. *In* Mankato: Its First Fifty Years, *Minnesota Historical Society*. RIGHT: Sheldon Barney, lawyer, land speculator, and probable member of the Knights of the Forest. *In* Mankato: Its First Fifty Years, *Minnesota Historical Society*

Though Asa is the only brother named as a Knights of the Forest member in the *Mankato Free Press*'s 1886 "Secret History" article, and Charles was living in Wisconsin at the time of the US–Dakota War, it is hard to imagine that Sheldon was not involved, or even a leader, in the Knights of the Forest. Sheldon and Asa pursued active professional, civic, and social lives in Mankato. Sheldon's partner, both at their law office and in most other enterprises, was John A. Willard. Meanwhile, Asa operated various businesses and was usually identified as a bookkeeper by occupation. According to *Mankato: Its First Fifty Years*, the brothers engaged in multiple industries over the years—with each other, on their own, or with other partners like Willard. It is uncertain if any of those businesses ever turned a profit, but Sheldon Barney and John A. Willard were the most well-known of all the profiteers for the fortune they made from Ho-Chunk land because it allowed them to stop working at other ventures. It was the basis for their wealth. The names of both the Barney brothers and of John A. Willard appear on patents issued by the US General Land Office for their purchase of Ho-Chunk lands. The Barney brothers and Willard, like Chapman, remained respected civic leaders in Mankato until their deaths. Asa attended a 1916 "Old Settlers Reunion," where historian Thomas Hughes interviewed an unnamed person about the Knights; Hughes briefly discussed the Knights in his *History of Blue Earth County and Biography of Its Leading Citizens.*[17]

There is a possibility that one or both Barney brothers were founding members of the Knights of the Forest. The 1886 "Secret History" article says there were "three persons, two of them citizens of Mankato, and one of Garden City, conversing about the situation, [and they] conceived the idea of forming a secret order, whose object should be the removal of all Indians from the State." Although Asa Barney moved to Mankato later in his life, his family homestead was near Garden City,

John A. Willard, business partner of Sheldon Barney. *In* **Mankato: Its First Fifty Years,** *Minnesota Historical Society*

An ad distributed by Willard and Barney, 1867. *Blue Earth County Historical Society* where he lived at the time of the US–Dakota War. But Sheldon, who also owned a homestead near Garden City while living and working in Mankato, is more likely the founding member from there. Chapman's 1916 newspaper article listed Chapman and Asa Barney as "members" and described Asa as being "initiated at Garden City." According to Thomas Hughes, the Knights were established in a "law office" in Block 14, which "was for years the only important business block of the town"; it was also the location of Sheldon Barney's and John A. Willard's law office. The masons, who held meetings there, probably observed the hanging of the thirty-eight Dakota men from that office.[18]

Sheldon and Asa were members of the masonic lodge as well as several other fraternal organizations in Mankato, including the Knights Templar and Independent Order of Odd Fellows. Sheldon conducted Odd Fellows rituals at the time capsule ceremony in 1866, and the capsule included other items pertaining to Sheldon's businesses, indicating that he contributed to its contents. He would thus have had the opportunity to add the Knights' "Ritual," a document of initiations deemed worthy of preservation as part of the city's history.

JOHN F. MEAGHER

Fraternal organizations and societies created interconnected social networks that functioned as sorting mechanisms for like-minded people. The more controversial the club's purposes and culture, the more "secret society" and less "fraternal order" they became. People joined organizations based on their religion, political leanings, or other business and social interests. Sometimes the groups offered a way for people to rise above other differences toward a common goal. For instance, Irish-Catholic immigrant John F. Meagher followed the papal ban on masonry and was not a member of the Mankato masons, but he was a very successful and active businessman in the community. A secret society like the Knights of the Forest could help him bridge the distinctions that might have otherwise limited his social and political relations with the other members who had masonic and Protestant backgrounds.[19]

John F. Meagher was among the most determined and prosperous moneymakers of all the Mankato entrepreneurs. He was born April 11, 1836, in County Kerry, Ireland, and immigrated to America in 1847, two years after the start of the Great Famine, living first for a few years on a farm in Illinois. When he was fourteen, he began work as a tinsmith apprentice in Illinois. He moved to Red Wing, Minnesota, before relocating permanently to Mankato in 1858. Three years later, he bought an existing hardware store. Over the next few decades, he acquired "a large private fortune." His store profited from

John F. Meagher, hardware store owner and member of the Knights of the Forest. *In* Mankato: Its First Fifty Years, *Minnesota Historical Society*

the temporary population boom as soldiers and other visitors stayed in Mankato in November and December 1862. Advertisements for Meagher's hardware store contained only a few lines of basic text in the spring of 1862. But by the fall of 1863, he was spending more on marketing in the *Mankato Record* and the *Mankato Independent*, and his ads now included a graphic: a sizable picture of a stove. A few years later, as farms in the area flourished, he was able to purchase the entire "Agricultural Column" in the newspaper. In 1897 he identified himself to the editor of the *Mankato Review* as a member of the Knights and provided a brief overview of the organization, which he ended with, "Many gentlemen now living in Mankato and Blue Earth County belonged to the Knights of the Forest."[20]

Meagher did not have quite the same background as the Barney brothers, the Porter family, or Charles A. Chapman. He was not born in America, nor was he a member of the masons. It is likely he was not overly familiar with secret societies or fraternal organizations, since he had spent his youth surviving a famine, immigrating, and apprenticing. He was a shrewd capitalist in Mankato, however, and the US–Dakota War was where he first made his mark and built a reputation. Meagher's biography does not credit the hardware store for his wealth. Apparently, he "was always active and alert in business enterprise, building many houses and acquiring much property." Much like Willard and Sheldon Barney, he "dealt largely and profitably in lands."[21]

His role as militiaman and member of the Knights of the Forest was likely part of his effort to integrate with the business culture. Frontier militias functioned as intercultural social clubs in the same way that fraternal organizations often spanned differences. During the US–Dakota War, he enlisted in the militia to fight at New Ulm and served as captain of the Mankato Home Guards. His participation in the Battle of New Ulm made him a local hero in Mankato, especially among

St. Peter and Paul Catholic Church, Mankato, about 1900. *Minnesota Historical Society*

members of St. Peter and Paul Catholic Church. In 1862 and the years that followed, Meagher worked to attain business partnerships and elected offices. He followed this wartime success with other business ventures like a woolen factory and real estate. He was an incorporator of the First National Bank of Mankato, then left and organized the Citizens' National Bank, and then served as president of the merged National Citizens' Bank until his death.[22]

The US–Dakota War, and likely the Knights of the Forest, launched Meagher into political and economic success, but his veteran status was also a big part of his identity. He was intimately involved with war commemoration and served on the commission to locate the New Ulm battle site, where he gave a speech at the dedication of a monument. Meagher is the only one of the four identified Knights men whose biography emphasizes his status in the militia.[23]

"Home guard" militias were local groups of men who did not formally enlist in the state militias; some were created before the US-Dakota War. The home guards continued to patrol around Mankato and other townsites through the fall of 1862, ostensibly for protection against the Ho-Chunk. Since John F. Meagher was the leader of the Mankato Home Guards and is a confirmed member of the Knights of the Forest, it is possible that the Knights of the Forest coordinated or collaborated with area militiamen. It is also possible that Knights of the Forest members populated the Mankato Home Guards and other militias near the reservation.

There is no record of the specific activities of the Mankato Home Guards beyond its muster roll, which also includes Chapman and Sheldon Barney. Thomas Hughes's history of Blue Earth County notes that no muster rolls exist for home

Winnebago Indian Agency, Blue Earth County, before 1863. *Photo by Benjamin F. Upton, Minnesota Historical Society*

guards formed at Garden City, Vernon, and Shelby, areas where the Porter and Barney families owned homesteads at the time. Militia groups had formed in those locations in 1859 and in 1861, and Garden City had maintained "a flourishing militia company" since 1857. In the days after the Battle of New Ulm, the Danville Home Guards formed near the reservation and "were stationed each night, and every move of the [Ho-Chunk] closely scrutinized . . . at the [Ho-Chunk] Agency, where the main body of the Indians were congregated." With all that paramilitary activity around the reservation, the Mankato Knights of the Forest Grand Lodge could have easily coordinated and operated militias with their subordinate lodges in those areas.[24]

Secret Societies and Political Activity in Nineteenth-Century America

The Knights of the Forest was only the newest iteration of Henry Dodge's Committee of Safety in Wisconsin and part of a long tradition of Western social political organization. In *A Secret Society History of the Civil War*, historian Mark Lause describes a distinct tradition of American fraternal orders based on a European model of freemasonry, which he calls the "oldest model of a secular voluntary organization," that "emerged . . . with unavoidable implications for the political organizations built in its wake and for the revolutionary movements of the eighteenth century." The tradesmen in Europe had formed organizations like the Freemasons for centuries, using secret hand signs or passwords to accommodate an illiterate membership (and to distinguish trade skills), but in the seventeenth and eighteenth centuries more affluent men began to join. The Freemasons eventually formed the Grand Lodge at London in 1717 as masonry spread throughout Europe and America. Members of masonic lodges pledged to put masonic interests before their religion, nation, or social class. The Roman Catholic Church forbade its members to join the masons, declaring that masonic teachings, rituals, and secrecy were antithetical to Catholic teachings; Catholic fraternal service organizations like the Knights of Columbus arose to fill their need for social groups.[25]

According to Lause, the further masonry spread from the reach of the Grand Lodge, the more predisposed the organization became to subversive political and social modifications. Even more alterations of the freemasonry model of fraternal orders came when transplanted revolutionaries from Europe brought the idea of secret societies to the United States in the late eighteenth century. The European example of secret fraternal organizations was reshaped and developed in early nineteenth-century America by labor groups in the Northeast; by religious, mutual aid, or benevolent societies; and by grassroots political movements. By the 1830s the idea of fraternal orders for political action had spread through the Midwest to Ohio and Michigan, where a secret society known as the Hunters Lodges participated in the Patriot War—a group of border skirmishes between the British and bands of Canadian refugees in the United States who wanted to overthrow British rule in Canada. The Hunters Lodges were among the earliest American secret societies that acted as a paramilitary organization for an expansionist political cause in the face of federal opposition. Then in the 1840s and 1850s, fraternal associations like the Brotherhood of the Union and the Universal Democratic Republicans, whose ranks and leadership were often made up of military members, veterans, and officers, provided both financial and militia assistance for their controversial political causes.[26]

In the decades before the US Civil War, Americans were absorbed with their desire for expansion based on the ideals of Manifest Destiny, and secret societies functioned more and more as social networks for political activity among white Protestant males. When expansionist settler-colonists encountered a problem in border regions of the country, local elites sometimes formed organizations like fraternal orders, councils, committees on safety, or secret societies that delivered political messages to the federal government both by their very existence and also literally, by sending petitions, letters, and resolutions. When these organizations focused on slavery or Native people, they occasionally functioned as a ready militia or paramilitary if the federal government did not respond adequately to their official messages. At the same time, federal officials encouraged local expansionist exploits on the frontier when it met the government's political and diplomatic needs.[27]

As the issue of slavery deepened sectional divides in the late 1850s, one southern secret society was formed with an explicit paramilitary purpose. The decade before the Civil War was the golden age of filibustering for expansion, and the rhetoric of these movements was increasingly about extension of slavery rather than territory. The notorious Knights of the Golden Circle, created in 1858 by George Bickley, is perhaps the best illustration of this shift. The group was dedicated to the expansion of slavery within a geographic area that stretched from Maryland to Oregon to South America. Lause describes Bickley as a "confidence man" who often moved around the border regions of America as his debts grew too large or people discovered he was a schemer. He created the secret society as a money-making venture that first focused on expansionist paramilitary expeditions before turning its ambitions toward secession and the buildup to the US Civil War.[28]

Organizations like the Freemasons, the Knights of the Golden Circle, and the Union of Brotherhood provided the social networks necessary for white men to coordinate solidarity for their privileged positions in early nineteenth-century American society. Lause characterizes this era as having a "paranoid style" that was marked by a transition into market capitalism, romanticism, and the high emotions of antebellum America. Bickley's propensity to skip town and successfully reinvent himself whenever his local social networks collapsed indicates he likely used the larger, more universal social structures provided by fraternal orders to advance in this era. As Lause says, Bickley was part of an entrepreneurial "growing acceptance that the young American man on the make had to become a kind of confidence man himself in order to succeed." The masons and other secret societies were located throughout America, and they allowed men on the move in the frontier to recognize like-minded strangers via their hand signs, rituals, or other symbols.[29]

The Knights of the Golden Circle is an early example of how secret societies functioned in controversial political movements. Their influence came in the form of the propaganda images that were created both for and against the group. Northerners feared them as the real-world "Slave Empire Conspiracy"; members played this reputation up or down, depending on their needs of the moment. The mystery around fraternal orders that billed themselves as secret societies allowed fluidity for men who wished to bend the story their way. Lause points out that secret societies used "smoke and mirrors to create the perception of scale," and Bickley knew that "the importance of any secret society turned largely on how it presented itself" in order to exert pressure on governments. Their power and influence resided in the impression that their particular threat existed, no matter the reality of the situation.[30]

Members of secret societies in the nineteenth century usually belonged to multiple political and social organizations. Many men who joined the Knights of the Golden Circle were in filibusterer or paramilitary groups like the Texas Rangers; some were politicians, and most belonged to other orders like the Freemasons, the Order of the Lone Star, and the Sons of Liberty, not to mention having roles in religious and trade groups. This kind of social web thrived on fraternal organizations whose military manifestations often took to mystery, intrigue, and secrecy to mask controversial or morally questionable martial motivations. Less provocative secret organizations like the Order of Odd Fellows or the Freemasons were common nineteenth-century fixtures throughout nearly all of America, especially at startup towns in the border regions, and Mankato was no exception. Lause points out that by this time, "fraternal hucksterism had become a sort of in-joke in which everyone seemed to be in the know." Such groups were considered an essential element to any successful pioneer town.[31]

New settlements in nineteenth-century America were vying for future economic power, and Mankato's founders were quick to set up the social structures needed to become a respectable city. Despite the settler-colonists' worries that the reservation would inhibit the area's growth, Mankato was what one historian described as an up-and-coming American "market town" and a "distributing center for goods" that was full of "economic opportunity." Ho-Chunk people also found opportunity there as the primary diggers of ginseng when it was among the top exports from the state. Fraternal orders were as key to the county's development as churches, businesses, and local governments. The masons were the only fraternal organization in Blue Earth County at the time of the US–Dakota War, but there were numerous others by the time Hughes wrote his history of the county in 1901. Ceremonies of any kind in Mankato, including anniversary parties, cornerstone dedications, and funerals, often incorporated the rites or rituals of fraternal organizations.[32]

The fraternal orders were a central part of identity for Mankato civic leaders and businessmen. In Hughes's history of the county, nearly all of the men's biographies include a list of their "fraternal relations." The word *fraternal* is mentioned over one hundred times in the biographical section, illustrating the importance of their association with these groups in their lives. Hughes also discusses the Knights of the Forest in his county history, but he does not attach any person's name to the organization nor provide any details beyond the existence of "sublodges" in nearby towns. Every account of the Knights of the Forest emphasizes that its members were local "prominent men." The four known members provide fine examples of their peers.[33]

Most of the known and suspected members of the Knights of the Forest had lived near the Ho-Chunk people for years, and they were undoubtedly aware of the Ho-Chunks' history with the United States. The government agents and white traders who lived on the reservation were part of the business community of Mankato; Chapman, Hughes, and other contemporary Mankato history writers mentioned them often. The trader Asa White married a Ho-Chunk woman, lived on the reservation, and was friends with John J. Porter Sr. White and his partner, Isaac Marks, owned a hardware store, a ginseng business, and several other business ventures. They also built a large stone building in Mankato in 1855 where Marks became the first masonic initiate and the Knights of the Forest later held meetings. Minnesota newspapers before and after the US–Dakota War often vilified reservation traders and agents, but not because they were swindling Native people. Instead, they accused traders of attempting to keep the reservations located in Minnesota for their own benefit. However, traders and agents like Henry Sibley—even though they often had mixed-ancestry children of their own—sometimes participated in anti-Indian militias or armies. White fought with the Mankato Home Guards during the war.[34]

Their strategy toward that end was to engage in typical nineteenth-century political activities. They held public meetings, sent "resolutions" to newspapers and legislatures, signed petitions, wrote editorials, and organized a grassroots society with mysterious paramilitary possibilities.[35]

7 THE KNIGHTS OF THE FOREST

With Mankato's local officials, businessmen, and general population among the four thousand who witnessed the execution of the condemned Dakota men in attendance, it is probable that the people who would become members of the Knights of the Forest were in attendance. Some later attested to their presence. In support of a soldier's request for compensation, Asa Barney, Charles A. Chapman, and John F. Meagher all signed a letter swearing that they had witnessed the hanging. In a history of the Mankato masons that Chapman published in 1902, he boasted that the Dakota prisoners were hanged "on the levee in full view from the windows of the Masonic Hall," where Knights of the Forest meetings were held. Asa Barney's obituary contained a full description of his exact location at the execution, including the position of his footing. And it is doubtful that John J. Porter Jr. and his father, John J. Porter Sr. – a local politician and the man for whom the Ho-Chunk removal camp was named – would have missed such a significant event in their hometown.[1]

Mob threats had pressured President Lincoln, and they must have had an impact on his decision to execute the Dakota. Settler-colonists could draw their own conclusions about how to push the government into a quick removal of the Ho-Chunk as well. A week after the hanging, on the same day the president issued the Emancipation Proclamation that ended slavery in the states that were "in rebellion against the United States," men in Mankato created an organization meant to extend the successful campaign against the Dakota to the Ho-Chunk.

The Founding

The 1886 "Secret History" newspaper article tells the founding story with great drama: "The date being the last of December, 1862, or the first of January 1863," when three persons — feeling that "the future prosperity of Mankato, and indeed of all this region, depended on obtaining the speedy removal of the Winnebagoes from our vicinity, and even from the state" — founded the Knights of the Forest, "a secret order, whose object should be the removal of all Indians from the State."

The founding of the secret order took place in Mankato, which was the headquarters of the Grand Lodge that took applications and issued charters to subordinate lodges. As its membership grew, the group met in a carpenter's shop, in an office in Block 14, in the Masonic Hall, and in other places: "They considered it expedient to move from place to place, lest they might attract attention by meeting many times in one building." Its membership, wrote historian Hughes, included "some of the most prominent and influential men in Mankato and Blue Earth County." Both the 1886 "Secret History" article and Hughes's county history mention the sublodges in Garden City and Meriden.[2]

The most valuable and immediate evidence of the Knights of the Forest is their four-page pamphlet of initiation rites and oath, entitled "Ritual," which is the only document known to have survived the organization (see Appendix C). There may have been proceedings, charters, and rosters that were forever lost: the 1886 "Secret History" article notes that the organization's records, including a constitution and by-laws, were destroyed in a fire. (It is possible they were in John F. Meagher's warehouse, which burned down some years after the war.) Chapman's 1916 article reports, "The ritual is still in existence, and the greatest of secrecy surrounded this little book and the lodge"; he may have been referring to the specific document placed in the time capsule in 1868 or to another copy.[3]

Nonetheless, the document he referred to provides some indication of the organization's political activities and mechanisms. The initiation rites and oath contain mostly political promises, leaving the impression that its members' impetus was simply to win elections. But the true motivation was land. The Knights saw the reservation as an obstacle to the region's progress and believed communities surrounding it would benefit if the lands owned by Ho-Chunk people were taken over by whites. The four known members clearly benefited. Chapman, the Harvard-educated land surveyor, and Asa Barney, whose brother Sheldon gave up his other ventures because there was "more money in [Ho-Chunk] lands," personally profited from Ho-Chunk removal. Chapman and Sheldon Barney both had real estate interests in the county for years before the war, and all four men purchased land patents on or near former reservation land after the removal.[4]

On January 21, 1863, about three weeks after the Knights of the Forest was founded, 685 Blue Earth County residents signed a petition addressed to President Lincoln and the secretary of the interior, who oversaw the Office of Indian Affairs (see Appendix D). The petition's text is a long quotation from a letter written by US senator Morton S. Wilkinson of Mankato to "Judge Cleveland"—probably Guy K. Cleveland, who had been a Faribault County judge before purchasing the *Mankato Independent*. It asserts that "The annuity of these Indians, although considerable, is not enough to keep them from starvation. . . . For years, they have been in the habit of wandering

Removal of the Winnebago Indians.

To the President of the United States and to the Secretary of the Interior—The undersigned, citizens of the State of Minnesota and residents of the country immediately adjacent to the Winnebago Reservation, respectfully represent and petition:

That the terrible events which have just transpired in this neighborhood clearly prove that the rich, productive counties surrounding the reservation must be vacated, and the pleasant homes which have cost so much privation and sacrifice, must be given up by those who now possess them, or the Indians must vacate their reservation. These people cannot longer remain in close proximity. The reason is apparent. These Indians are now located upon a small reservation, about eighteen miles in length by nine in breadth; there is but little game upon this tract, and by the terms of the treaty they must remain upon it. The annuity of these Indians, although considerable, is not sufficient to keep them from starvation. Their idle, dissolute habits prevent their performing any useful labor, and hence, for years, they have been in the habit of wandering over the adjacent country, plundering the occupants of the ceded territory, and committing depredations upon the people wherever they went. With a marvelous patience the people have for years submitted to their annoyance, and perhaps they might have longer remained quiet but for the horrid massacre in their midst, which, from its sudden violence and brutality shocked and alarmed the people of the entire State. Henceforth the Indians cannot be permitted to leave their reservation, and to be confined to it, is starvation, for they will not work. Hence the removal of the Indians is a necessity. Humanity requires it; the welfare of the Indians, as well as the peace of the whites demand it." Letter of Hon. M. S. Wilkinson to Judge Cleveland.

We therefore most respectfully ask that the Winnebago tribe of Indians be immediately removed beyond the borders of our State.

A petition signed by 685 Blue Earth County residents. *National Archives* over the adjacent country, plundering the occupants of the ceded territory. . . . Perhaps they [the settler-colonists] might have longer remained quiet" but for the US–Dakota War.

The petition demanded the "removal of the Winnebago Indians" because "the peace of the whites demand it."[5]

The settler-colonists surrounding the reservation had never been silent about their desire to have the Ho-Chunk people removed. The debate had taken place in the Mankato press for years, and this was not the first petition that asked for Ho-Chunk removal from Blue Earth County. The 1886 "Secret History" article noted this ear-

Morton S. Wilkinson, probably 1860s. *Photo by Mathew Brady, Smithsonian Institution*

lier activity: "It was, however, a difficult project owing to the great influence with the government of those whose interest it was to have them remain." This presumably meant the agents and Indian traders who profited from their presence.[6]

Senator Morton Wilkinson was a Republican. John J. Porter Sr., the Barneys, Chapman, and Meagher were all staunch Democrats. It is reasonable to think that the Democratic-leaning members of the Knights of the Forest, despite their political rivalries, circulated a Republican-led petition at their meetings. The Knights of the Forest's oath, taken by Democratic politicians John F. Meagher and John J. Porter Sr., emphasized the promise to vote for candidates sympathetic to the removal cause. The Knights meant to provide an organization that would connect men from different partisan affiliations to work toward the goal of Ho-Chunk removal. The 1886 "Secret History" article said the three founders of the Knights "believed that by uniting men of both political parties to work for a common object, throwing over their proceedings the mysterious veil of secrecy," they would have more influence. Still, the only signature of a probable Knights of the Forest member on the petition is that of E. D. B. Porter.[7]

Of course, nearly all Minnesota politicians were supportive of the Knights' goals in the early months of 1863. John Wise's Democratic newspaper, the *Mankato Record*, was in fierce competition with the Republican *Mankato Independent* as to which party was anti-Indian in the correct way; that battle had been going on for years in Mankato, but it intensified in 1862.[8]

A separate petition circulated by Brown County men in January 1863 responded to critics on the East Coast by asking the US government to move the Ho-Chunk people to parks in Philadelphia. Wise's *Mankato Record* said this was "carrying a joke too far" and condemned "its tone and character" for being "disrespectful to the communities named therein," even though the *Record* had repeatedly printed calls for "removal or extermination" of "all Indians." Wise wrote that "a petition respectful and earnest in request and language" would be much more effective and the Brown County petitioners should not have "intermeddled in our local affairs." Presumably, this more "respectful" petition was Wilkinson's, but the Democrat John Wise probably would not have publicly admitted as much.[9]

At least one signature of a prominent Democrat appears on Wilkinson's petition, that of longtime Mankato businessman Daniel Buck. He later served as Blue Earth County attorney, a Minnesota Supreme Court justice, a state legislator for the Mankato area, and a member of the Minnesota State Normal School Board. Buck was in the same political, social, and business circles as Meagher, Chapman, the Barneys, and Willard. He was involved with the First National and Citizens' National Banks along with John F. Meagher. Chapman's biography states that he surveyed Buck's South Bend land in 1858. A Mankato history described Buck as a "noble specimen of American manhood," and he was often the speaker for public events in Mankato. Late in his life, the Democrat Daniel Buck gave the oratory at the dedication ceremony for a monument to the deceased Republican senator Morton Wilkinson. His signature on this document suggests that his social and business ties brought him close to the leaders of the Knights; he may also have been a member.[10]

Even though removal was a bipartisan effort, no evidence has yet identified any Republican members of the Knights of the Forest. Many non-Republicans signed Wilkinson's petition for removal

Daniel Buck, about 1900. *Minnesota State University, Mankato*

Citizens' National Bank and Star Clothing House, South Front Street, Mankato, 1881. *Blue Earth County Historical Society*

in January 1863 along with Daniel Buck and E. D. B. Porter. Thomas Hughes never tied E. D. B. to a political party, but he was probably a relative of John J. Porter Sr., who was elected to the state legislature as a Democrat. Several other locally known but politically unaffiliated men appear on the petition, like Josiah Whipple, Harvey Burgess, Judge Lorin Cray, and Reuben Butter. A secret society like the Knights of the Forest would have been a reasonable political-action outlet for someone like E. D. B., who may have socialized with both Republicans and Democrats but was not necessarily politically associated. The Knights might have also been attractive to people like Judge Buck, who was friendly with Republicans and could maybe even recruit some into the organization.[11]

The "Ritual" document of the Knights of the Forest displays the singularity of its objective as well as its members' fearmongering political opportunism. It lays out no goals, questions, promises, or statements pertaining to any subject other than "Indian removal." The politicians in Porter Sr. and Meagher must have been especially mindful of the part where members took an oath to "sacrifice every political and other preference to accomplish" their goals. Each member vowed that he would "not aid or assist in any manner to elect to office in this state or the United States any person outside this order, who will not publicly or privately pledge himself" to the removal of Indians from Minnesota. The known Knights of the Forest in the Mankato Lodge were Democrats. However, the careful phrasing of the oath left the door open for Republicans to join, since their candidates were just as anti-Indian as the opposing Democrats.[12]

In 1916 Charles A. Chapman described the Knights' recruitment techniques in his signed article, "Secret Society of Early Mankato." When a person was "known to be in sympathy with the objects of the order he was approached by a member,

RITUAL.

OPENING.

[When the hour arrives for opening the Lodge, the Worthy Chancellor (and in his absence the Worthy Vice Chancellor) will take the chair and call the Lodge to order by giving one rap.]

Worthy Chancellor. The officers will take their stations. The Conductor will see that the Lodge is guarded in a proper manner. The Conductor will examine those present, that all may be worthy.

[If any are present without the pass word, they must leave the room.

C. [Reports to W. C.]

W. C. [The chancellor gives three raps, all the members rise.]

Officers and members : The objects for which we are assembled, are worthy of our cause. It is no less than the preservation of our lives, our families, and our homes. Let us be ever watchful and keep constantly in mind the sacred obligation which binds us together as brothers in one common interest. I sincerely hope this meeting may be profitable to each one of us, and that we may go forth from this Lodge stronger and braver in the determination to banish forever from our beautiful State every Indian who now desecrates our soil.

W. C. The Worthy Vice Chancellor will now open this Lodge.

W. V. C. By direction of our worthy Chancellor, I declare this Lodge open for the transaction of business, and for extending universal opposition to all tribes of Indians in the State of Minnesota.

[The W. C. gives one rap and the members take their seats.]

W. C. The Financial secretary will call the roll of members.

INITIATION.

[When the Lodge is ready for initiation the F. S. will retire with the Assistant Conductor, to collect the initiation fee, when the A. C. shall propound to the candidate the following questions :]

C. Before you can proceed any further, you must give your assent to the following questions.

Question. Do you promise upon your honor that you will keep all secrets and information which I may here reveal to you?

Answer. I do.

Question. Are you in favor of the removal of all tribes of Indians from the State of Minnesota ?

Answer. I am.

Question. Will you sacrifice all political and other preferences to accomplish that object ?

Answer. I will.

Question. Will you do all in your

The first page of the Knights of the Forest's "Ritual." *Minnesota State University, Mankato* who in the course of conversation asked him casually what he would think of the formation of a society. . . . The prospective candidate was carefully sounded, so that he might not even know of the lodge should he back down." The recruit would be invited to a meeting "to discuss this proposition," where he was met by a committee. "Not till he was questioned by the committee sent out for that purpose did it dawn on him that he was entering an established lodge." A surprise initiation into the group then took place. The newcomer would swear an oath, stating:

> I _____, of my own free will and accord, in the full belief that every Indian should be removed from the state, by the memory of the inhuman cruelties perpetrated upon defenseless citizens, and in the presence of the members of this order here assembled, do most solemnly promise, without any mental reservation whatever, to use every exertion and influence in my power to cause the removal of all tribes of Indians from the State of Minnesota.

Members were instructed "to remember that one of the great duties of your life is not only to advocate the banishment of all Indians from this state, but to prevail on others to do so." This rite of passage probably took place dozens of times, given the multiple chapters throughout the county.[13]

The Knights justified the organization's existence as a fight for their very survival. During initiation, the "Worthy Vice Chancellor" reminded recruits that many lives had been lost to the Dakota and declared "the white man and the Indians cannot dwell together in peace and harmony." New initiates were commended because they had "chosen the only path which will give security and safety to the future and prevent the blow of the glittering knife and merciless tomahawk."[14]

Their ceremonial promises, oaths, and goals focused on a generic image of an "Indian." This terminology and the battle imagery contained in their oath combines the Dakota and

Ho-Chunk people into one enemy group. In fact, if the initiation rites and oath contained in the "Ritual" document were studied independently from the newspaper articles or any other information about the organization, it could seem as though the group had targeted the already interned Dakota people. The recruits vowed that they would not rest until the entire "accursed race of infuriated demons" was "driven far away towards the setting sun."[15]

The authors of the Knights' "Ritual" probably used the term "all Indians" intentionally. It is likely that they did favor the removal of "all Indians" from the state, which would have included the Ojibwe in the north. They may also have been leaving the door open for an expansion of the Knights to the northern part of the state, or anywhere else that Indigenous people lived. And identifying the peaceable Ho-Chunk people with the Dakota people who had recently participated in hostilities was an argument for removal.

The initiation rite contains a promise of confidentiality, and the newspaper articles emphasize the secrecy of the group. Secret societies with a paramilitary or violent association use intrigue and mystery as a sort of dark attempt to influence people and officials through implied or real threats. The late nineteenth-century Ku Klux Klan needed the confidentiality of a secret society, especially when Klan members were supported by the law enforcers of the area, because they advocated and engaged in illegal activities like lynching. Members of the Knights may have desired secrecy to protect their reputations, although it is unlikely they were ashamed to have such opinions in 1863 Minnesota. Although Chapman's newspaper articles stress the Knights' goal to pressure the government, members may have sought secrecy at least in part because they, too, advocated unlawful and inhumane activities, such as shooting any Ho-Chunk person found off their reservation.

In addition, secrecy would allow them to *seem* to have a larger membership. The 1886 "Secret History" article emphasizes the Knights' goal of government pressure. Members knew a mysterious organized threat would "wield more power than by working openly with a petition." Like all secret societies in the nineteenth century, "Its prestige was magnified in the minds of the people, and of the government, by the secrecy thrown around its proceedings." The article claims that the "mystery had its effect on the government, and it is very probable that without it the removal of the Indians might have been delayed for years." (Mankato leaders knew very well that the war meant the Ho-Chunk would eventually leave. The problem for the Knights was that it would not happen fast enough, which is why the article proudly says they prevented the *delay* of the removal.) In 1916, Chapman explained precisely how the secret society functioned in its political movement for forced relocation of the Ho-Chunk Nation: "Notwithstanding the oath of secrecy, hints of the organization got out and went even to government circles in Washington, exaggerated, of course, as they traveled until the U.S. Government began to take notice, for many in congress believed that a general uprising of the people of southern Minnesota was imminent, for the purpose of massacring the whole tribe of Winnebagoes."[16]

Over the years, the people of Mankato had signed petitions, held meetings, and sent letters asking the federal government to move the Ho-Chunk out of Minnesota. They had exhausted every conceivable argument for removal. The US–Dakota War finally gave them the advantage they needed to convince the federal government. The Knights, then, put forward a threat of mass violence under the guise of wartime fear that the federal government could not ignore.

Violence at Blue Earth in 1862 and 1863

The war brought the Ho-Chunk people threats of slaughter by their neighbors between September 1862 and May 1863. The federal agent to the Ho-Chunk, Saint Andre Durand Balcombe, wrote that whites had informed him the Ho-Chunk "will be massacred if they go out of their own country," so he had stationed soldiers at the agency and was attempting to keep the Ho-Chunk within the reservation.[17]

The threats were not empty. In September 1862, as the Dakota War was coming to a close, Balcombe reported that "A [Ho-Chunk man] was killed while crossing the Mississippi River, for no other reason than that he was an Indian."[18]

"Such is the state of public opinion," Balcombe continued, "that the murderer went unpunished." Although this happened nearly one hundred miles from Blue Earth County, it reflected a statewide danger to Native people. After the assassination of the Ojibwe leader Hole in the Day in June 1868, one northern Minnesota settler-colonist later stated, "If we did kill anybody in those days, it was no crime; you couldn't hang a man for killing ten Indians."[19]

Various militia and ad hoc guardsmen groups existed in Mankato, throughout Blue Earth County, and at the Ho-Chunk agency during the US–Dakota War. But all government-sanctioned militias had been mustered out of service by the time the Knights were established in January 1863. John F. Meagher's Mankato Home Guard defended Mankato and its vicinity, so perhaps some of those men refocused their energies on the Knights of the Forest.[20]

It is unclear if the function of US soldiers posted at the agency throughout the winter of 1862–63 was to guard the settlers or the Ho-Chunk people—or just keep the peace. Balcombe said the Ho-Chunk people were uneasy with the nearby hostility, and the arrival of soldiers led by Captain

Alonzo Edgerton had "allayed their fears to a great extent and also allayed to some extent the fears of the surrounding white people." However, Thomas Hughes noted that these soldiers were just as antagonistic as the settler-colonists toward the

Ho-Chunk people. He paraphrased their sentiments with disapproval: "That the only way to avoid Indian massacres was to massacre all the Indians" and "That the Indian had no rights the white man need respect."[21]

Despite the militant mob culture in Mankato at the time, there are no known reports of organized attacks on the Ho-Chunk reservation other than vague insinuations by Chapman. Official companies of US soldiers stationed at the Ho-Chunk agency and townsites near the reservation during and

Captain Alonzo Edgerton, about 1875. Photo by Zimmerman and Whitstruck, Minnesota Historical Society

after the US–Dakota War only reported boredom during the winter of 1862–63, except for the executions in Mankato.[22]

The 1886 "Secret History" is the only newspaper article that alludes to violent actions organized by the Knights. It states that the "business transacted" by the Knights can be easily understood by reading the order's oath. But the author adds:

> One noteworthy act of the Mankato Lodge, however, merits particular attention. This was the employment of a certain number of men whose duty was to lie in ambush on the outskirts of the Winnebago Reservation, and shoot any Indian who might be observed outside the lines. It is not the province

of this sketch to relate how many, if any, Indians were thus disposed of. It is sufficient to say that the designated parties went out on their scouting excursions, and in due time returned and reported. For obvious reasons their reports were not made a matter of record.[23]

It is still not clear if the Knights of the Forest planned to massacre the Ho-Chunk people, or if they just wanted everyone to think as much. Neither the "Ritual" nor the petition makes an outright call for armed action. Even if the newspaper article's account of "excursions" to the reservation is true, the top priority for the Knights was removal from the prime farmland. They had no concern for the hundreds of Ho-Chunk lives that would be lost. In fact, some members clearly viewed Ho-Chunk deaths as an added benefit after the war. One 1867 descriptive pamphlet marketing Mankato for settlement (and also Sheldon Barney's real estate business) said the Ho-Chunk had left Blue Earth County, probably to "utter extinction," but "nobody cares where."[24]

By the time the Knights of the Forest convened for the first time in January 1863, only a few hundred Dakota men remained in the Mankato prison, while most Dakota people were at Fort Snelling. Chapman's personal account of the society specifically mentions the goal of evicting the "Winnebago"; he mentions no other tribal nation. The Knights were not concerned with the Ojibwe who continued to live in the northern half of the state. Rather, they wanted the Ho-Chunk people who possessed valuable farmland near their own homes to leave so they could occupy that land without "annoyance."[25]

Very little documentation exists for activities at the Blue Earth County reservation from January through April 1863, the months when the Knights of the Forest was operational. There is a curious absence of agency letters from these months. Most information from Agent Balcombe from 1862 is in his annual report. According to Ho-Chunk claims filed against the government in 1931, the army held them in captivity the winter following the US–Dakota War before forcing their removal at gunpoint in the spring. When the Ho-Chunk leader Winneshiek and about 750 of his followers refused to leave, retreating to Lake Elysian in the north of the reservation, soldiers pursued them and compelled them to join the others at Camp Porter.[26]

Agent Balcombe's letters and contemporary newspaper articles attest that, despite threats from hostile neighbors, the Ho-Chunk wanted to stay on their Blue Earth County reservation—or, preferably, to return to their homeland of Wisconsin, where they knew anti-Indian sentiment among whites was equally strong. They had no desire to move farther from their ancestral home to uninhabitable land. When Ho-Chunk leader Baptiste LaSallier saw their newly designated reservation on the Missouri River in present-day South Dakota, he told the agent he was willing to risk the unfriendly white neighbors in Minnesota over the barren wasteland of Crow Creek, saying, "We are not afraid to die, but we do not wish to die here."[27]

8 THE BANISHMENT OF THE HO-CHUNK FROM MINNESOTA

It is unclear if the Ho-Chunk people living on the Blue Earth reservation were aware that the Knights of the Forest existed, but they were certainly alert to the danger of nearby whites. By the end of 1862, Agent Balcombe reported that they could no longer dig ginseng outside of the reservation boundaries or go into the neighboring towns to conduct business without fearing for their safety.

The Office of Indian Affairs approved funds for farm implements in the fall of 1862, but Henry Rice and Alexander Ramsey promptly intervened to have the funds canceled. They reasoned that the excitement of the settler-colonists meant the Ho-Chunk would surely be leaving, and there was no point in making permanent arrangements for their continued stay in Minnesota. Balcombe must have agreed, because he pointed to incidents like the Mississippi River murder and requested enough money to provide Ho-Chunk subsistence over the winter so they would not have to risk their lives leaving the reservation for food. In January Sibley sent another letter to the secretary of the interior with the same warning: Ho-Chunk people were forced to take dangerous chances outside the reservation to avoid starvation. Rice and Ramsey proved correct in their assumptions. Morton Wilkinson first introduced a bill in Congress to remove the Ho-Chunk on December 16, 1862, before the introduction of a Dakota removal bill and preceding the creation of the Knights of the Forest.[1]

Despite the dangers posed by hostile neighbors, Ho-Chunk people fought hard to keep their reservation in Blue Earth County. Many were upset when the agent informed them that settler-colonists were asking Congress for their removal because it was "very unjust under the circumstances, for they have become attached to this location, and would not leave it willingly, and think their fidelity ought to entitle them to respect and kind treatment." Winneshiek, who had previously protested a treaty that forced the reservation into allotments, adapted to the shifting conditions and changed his stance on the 1859 allotment treaty. He now wanted the allotments to be made final immediately, so individuals would receive permanent titles to their individual acreages. Thomas Hughes claimed that some Ho-Chunk people blamed Winneshiek for the removal because he had so fiercely opposed and blocked the allotment treaty's enactment. According to one Mankato newspaper article, Ho-Chunks on the reservation also arrested a white man for advocating their removal. They held him for a time before turning him over and then threatened the arrest of two others for the same advocacy, including the trader Asa White. Some Ho-Chunk families went to the courthouse to apply for US citizenship to keep their allotments. The judge promptly denied them and arrested Marcus Moore, the white man assisting them, for his effort.[2]

Government records reveal very little communication from the agency during the three months the Knights were active, so it is uncertain what direct effects the men "lying in ambush" at the reservation had on the Ho-Chunk people. The confinement to the reservation under hostile conditions that were worse than any experienced in Wisconsin must have produced an unhappy situation. The roll call counts during the Ho-Chunks' transport to South Dakota show that possibly a quarter of the population did leave over the winter, probably returning to Wisconsin—where settler-colonists still complained to the Indian Office of their presence. The *Winona Daily Republican* reported on May 18, 1863, that about twenty Ho-Chunk people passed through town on their way to Wisconsin. This group of Ho-Chunk likely never arrived in Mankato for the census counts, and others probably didn't either.[3]

The only letter from Agent Balcombe to his superiors in the early months of 1863 describes his work toward getting the Ho-Chunk reservation ready to move. His long letter details each of his activities toward the relocation of the reservation but makes no mention of the condition or disposition of the Ho-Chunk people. Balcombe, like most government officials in 1863, had been the focus of immense criticism since the US–Dakota War. The Democratic *Mankato Record* accused Republicans and their chosen Ho-Chunk agent, Balcombe, of supporting the reservation's existence in Blue Earth County.[4]

Furthermore, both Asa White and the *Record* claimed Balcombe was stealing from the Ho-Chunk. Almost forty years later, Hughes noted:

> It seems that in the distribution of the last goods sent by the government to this county for the Winnebagoes, 1,420 blankets had been sent, but only 500 were delivered to the Indians; 1150 yards of blue cloth sent, only 275 yards delivered; 990 yards of gray cloth sent, only 330 yards delivered; 2756 yards of plaid linsey sent, none delivered; 2860½ yards of cloth sent, none delivered; four dozen plaid wool shawls sent, none delivered; three dozen extra blanket shawls sent, none delivered. The goods not delivered were estimated as worth $10,000. . . . Many of the employees and others thought it no sin to steal from Indians. This is but a sample of what was being done at every Agency and at most every payment.[5]

Corruption in the Indian Office was widespread and well known across the country. Appointments as agents were political plums, awarded to supporters who could then skim from payments and award contracts on condition of kickbacks. For his part, Balcombe claimed White was holding a grudge over the revocation of his trader license. White and his partner Isaac Marks had followed the Ho-Chunk as traders for years alongside government agents and other traders like Henry Rice, who had nearly all been appointed and licensed by Democratic presidents and governors. But when Republicans Abraham Lincoln and Alexander Ramsey were elected to the presidency and Minnesota governorship, respectively, in 1860, Republican loyalists replaced the Democrats in political patronage positions, like Indian agents. Some agents, including Balcombe, extended the political cronyism to trader licensure and promptly refused to license long-standing traders who were Democratic partisans, like Asa White and Isaac Marks. At the time Balcombe wrote the letter in May 1863, he was probably fatigued from a long winter among white neighbors who were hostile to both him and the Ho-Chunk. Yet he expressed more concern for his reputation than he did for the security of Ho-Chunk people.[6]

The Treaty of 1859 had included a clause allowing the president to alter its terms "in such manner and to whatever extent he may judge to be necessary and expedient for [the Ho-Chunks'] welfare and best interest." On February 23, 1863, the US Congress passed an act ordering the Ho-Chunk to leave Blue Earth County for the Crow Creek Reservation in South Dakota. The *Mankato Independent* proclaimed, "Glorious News!" and the Ho-Chunk people were expelled from Minnesota in the spring of 1863. With no justification for the government to compel removal on the Ho-Chunk people other than the fervent anti-Indian sentiment among nearby whites, it seems that the Knights of the Forest had achieved their desired effect. Starting on May 5, soldiers began forcing the Ho-Chunk to move to Camp Porter on the bank of the Minnesota River in Mankato behind the Hubbard Mill (now Ardent Mills) and await transportation.[7]

The only accounts of Camp Porter come from the Mankato newspapers. Ho-Chunk people would not be confined to the camp under threat of death in the city, as they had been on the reservation the previous nine months. Or at least they didn't act like it. They visited shops and were seen viewing the scaffolding where Dakota prisoners had been hanged. However, as soldiers forced more Ho-Chunk into Camp Porter over four days, Mankatoans became increasingly uneasy. Within a few

The south bank of the Minnesota River in Mankato, before 1919. This was probably the site of Camp Porter. The Hubbard Mill is in the background. *Photo by George E. Keene, Blue Earth County Historical Society*

The *Favorite*, one of the three steamboats that carried the Ho-Chunk
to Crow Creek, at Winona in 1861. *Minnesota Historical Society*

days, the newspapers began to describe Ho-Chunk presence as
an occupation of their city.[8]

On May 9, 1863, twelve hundred Ho-Chunk people and all
their belongings were packed onto three steamboats with soldiers to carry them down the Minnesota River.

Some Ho-Chunk people in Blue Earth County fought the
removal from Minnesota until the bitter end. A Mankato
paper reported that many families had already planted crops
for the year and "actually shed tears" at the prospect of leaving
them behind. Winneshiek and his band of 750 people refused
to leave their Lake Elysian village, so a company of soldiers
forced them into Mankato at gunpoint. They arrived at Camp
Porter on May 12 before thirty-nine soldiers brought them
down the river to follow the same long journey.[9]

The Ho-Chunk stayed briefly at Fort Snelling. From there,
they were further tightly packed onto two steamships before
being transferred to a train, and then taken on a final boat ride
up the Missouri River to South Dakota.[10]

Years later, a Ho-Chunk man named John Blackhawk told Thomas Hughes that during their removal from the county in May 1863, the Ho-Chunk endured "ruffian soldiers. Women and girls raped, men murdered, and all subjected to every insult and indignity that brutal men could invent." Federal soldiers charged with Ho-Chunk removal were reportedly from Company One of the Tenth Regiment of Minnesota, primarily recruited from other Minnesota counties. Hughes claimed that the necessities of wartime allowed the enlistment of soldiers who were "scum . . . profane, drunken, vicious types" and "took advantage of their opportunity to commit all kinds of crimes" against the Ho-Chunk people on their journey to South Dakota.[11]

Coming Thunder Winneshiek and other leaders, probably photographed in May 1863 at the Fort Snelling camp. *Photo by Benjamin F. Upton, Minnesota Historical Society*

It took both the Ho-Chunk and the Dakota about a week to get to South Dakota, where there was nothing for them. Conditions in Crow Creek were appalling. The Dakota agent reported three or four deaths a day during the first six weeks at Crow Creek, totaling about 150 deaths. Ho-Chunk families took some Dakota women into their homes, sharing what little they had. The agents for both groups failed them in the summer of 1863, allowing their meat to rot and being overly confident in the success of crops in such a desolate region. Ho-Chunk men immediately began making trips to the Omaha Reservation in Nebraska—near where they had asked to be moved in 1846. Their time in South Dakota only brought them suffering, starvation, and death.[12]

There was so much suffering there that most Ho-Chunk people soon made their way down the Missouri River to live near the Omaha, another Siouan-speaking people. In 1865, they negotiated a treaty to purchase half the Omaha Reservation, which is where the Nebraska Tribe of Winnebago reservation is today. Because there was no census taken of Ho-Chunk in Wisconsin until 1874, it is difficult to know how many died in 1863 and 1864. Ho-Chunk historian Amy Lonetree estimates about 550 Ho-Chunk people died on the journey from Minnesota to Crow Creek.[13]

Ho-Chunk people never abandoned their collective desire to live on their original homeland in present-day Wisconsin. Over the years, Ho-Chunk resilience and determination to return seemed only to strengthen each time the federal government forced them to move. Some people never left Wisconsin, and many of those who left to live at the various reservations eventually went back. Some Ho-Chunks moved back and forth between Wisconsin and wherever the government reservation was located at the time. Over the years, agents at all five Ho-Chunk reservations received numerous letters from Wisconsin settler-colonists requesting the removal of Ho-Chunk people who were living in the nearby woods. In 1871, US soldiers forced more than one thousand Wisconsin Ho-Chunk into boxcars at gunpoint. The train then brought them to the reservation in Nebraska, where only 860 Ho-Chunk people arrived. A final effort by the military to evict them from Wisconsin came in 1874, with the same outcome as the previous attempts. Some Ho-Chunk people would never leave their homelands.[14]

Wakanjaxeriga, holding a long-stemmed pipe, stands behind other Ho-Chunk men on a visit to Wisconsin governor Lucius Fairchild, about 1866. Left to right: Yellow Thunder; his brother Wau-So-Mo-Ne-Ka (Hail-stone); Spoon-De-Kaury (son of Scha-Chip-Ka-Ka); Nes-Ka-Ka (Whitewater); and Chou-Ga-Ga (grandson of Scha-Chip-Ka-Ka). *Photo by James F. Bodtker, Wisconsin Historical Society, WHI-125739*

Meanwhile, the groups that lived on the government reservations were repeatedly moved to places where they were unhappy. When they finally arrived at Blue Earth County, a place outside Wisconsin that they could tolerate, they were exiled from it to a place even more undesirable than the despised Long Prairie reservation. The Ho-Chunk even made one last effort for a government-sanctioned return to their homeland when they met General Henry Sibley's military expedition on their way to Crow Creek. Ho-Chunk leaders asked the general for a reservation in Wisconsin with American soldiers to guard them from hostile whites. Sibley saw the unfairness of their situation and implored the government to treat them justly, without necessarily endorsing their request. By this time, Minnesotans were more concerned with the US Civil War and expeditions against Dakota fugitives. Injustices against the Ho-Chunk were at the bottom of their priority list.[15]

On May 15, 1863, three days after the expulsion of the last Ho-Chunk people from Blue Earth County, the *Mankato Independent* announced the "Departure of the Winnebagoes" on one page, and "Valuable Land For Sale"—identified as "Winnebago Trust Lands"—on another page.[16]

There is, of course, no record of how the Knights of the Forest marked the success of their efforts. Perhaps they bestowed some additional honor on John J. Porter Sr., or maybe they performed some closing ceremony. The 1886 "Secret History" newspaper article notes the end of the Knights of the Forest as it justifies telling the group's secrets: "There is no betrayal of trust in publishing these activities now since the object for which the order was constituted having been accomplished, and the order itself having ceased forever, the people are now among those who, in the language of their ritual, are 'entitled to know the same.'"[17]

9 ETHNIC CLEANSING AND THE FORGOTTEN LEGACY

The Knights of the Forest was essentially a grassroots hate group engaged in ethnic cleansing of 1863 Blue Earth County, Minnesota, to support America's enthrallment with expansion, which most frontier settler-colonists believed to be the nation's Manifest Destiny. Many scholars and historians of ethnic cleansing and genocide have documented the function of local elites in advancing the societal goals of a dominant culture.

The nineteenth-century Ku Klux Klan was similar to the Knights of the Forest with its secret society influences and its purpose of racial terror. The Klan was responsible for thousands of lynchings, and its members terrorized Black families in their homes for decades. But the post–Civil War Ku Klux Klan was most concerned with maintaining political and social authority over Black Southerners who comprised their indispensable labor force. The Klan did not work toward a goal of ethnic cleansing. The Knights of the Forest seemed much more confident in their localized social and political power, and the state's Indigenous peoples served no economic purpose for them. So they focused on physical eradication of "all Indians" from their midst. This is why the Knights of the

Forest have more in common with organizations that affected ethnic cleansing, such as one in nineteenth-century Texas.

In *The Conquest of Texas: Ethnic Cleansing in the Promised Land, 1820–1875*, historian Gary Clayton Anderson recounts the role of the Texas Rangers in the struggle for land between Anglos and Natives. The Rangers have become a romanticized and celebrated institution in present-day America, but they have their origins in racism, greed, atrocities, and mass death. Anderson writes about a "culture of violence" that existed in mid-nineteenth-century Texas, in which both Indigenous people and Texans participated. But he points out that whites formed a policy and strategy around "racial violence" that "gradually led to the deliberate ethnic cleansing" of Comanche, Kiowa, and Apache peoples in Texas.

Although the Knights certainly never reached the levels of violence committed by the Rangers, their goals were the same. Colin Flint's geographic explanation of hate groups in *Spaces of Hate: Geographies of Discrimination and Intolerance in the U.S.A.* shows that the distinctions between such organizations are influenced by local conditions. The important difference for the Knights in Mankato, the event that may have halted the wholesale massacre of Ho-Chunk people, was the almost immediate banishment of the Ho-Chunk from the state. Without the relatively quick exile from Minnesota after the US–Dakota War, the Knights of the Forest membership could have enacted the same gradual, deliberate, genocidal ethnic cleansing that happened in Texas. Anderson points out that the early Texans would have been satisfied if the Indians had simply left. But—not surprisingly—the Indigenous people of Texas refused to leave their homelands without a fight. And so the Rangers became a paramilitary group, given complete discretion for what they saw as the protection of Texans. The Rangers were so successful that they were eventually put on the federal payroll.[1]

The Knights had the same goal and were prepared to use all the tools at their disposal to remove the Ho-Chunk from neighboring land under the guise of public safety. The Knights had involvement and support from Minnesota legislators such as John J. Porter Sr. and John F. Meagher. They also had militia connections through John F. Meagher and his Mankato Home Guard. The Knights could have spread across the state and transitioned to a publicly funded paramilitary hate group like the Rangers had the US-Dakota War continued long enough to grow the organization further. It is not hard to imagine the home guards being paid by the state to continue to fight the "Indian Wars" while federal soldiers engaged in the US Civil War. Governor Ramsey showed his willingness to use tax dollars to kill Indigenous people when he famously put a bounty on Dakota people.

While the Rangers were not a fraternal order or secret society like the Knights, they were like the Minnesota men in other, more dangerous ways. Anderson cites studies in Yugoslavia that show "Political elites often direct the actions of paramilitary groups involved in ethnic cleansing." He points out that many politicians had been Rangers and used Indian extermination as political rallying cries. Even though Rangers sometimes acted on their own, all of the Rangers who "forced removal or committed the occasional genocidal act were an extension of the Texas political system." The Knights were also connected to the state political system, with Sheldon Barney, John F. Meagher, and John J. Porter Sr. in the legislature before, during, and after the US-Dakota War and also likely members of the Mankato Grand Lodge. The Knights clearly functioned as a paramilitary group in a process of ethnic cleansing. If Chapman's allusions to murders during "excursions" were real occurrences, the Knights may have committed Texas Rangers-style atrocities.[2]

While it remains unknown if any member of the Knights

of the Forest ever murdered a Ho-Chunk person under the direction or protection of the organization, a massacre is not necessary to meet the conditions for ethnic cleansing and genocide. Hundreds of Ho-Chunk people died because of their removal from Minnesota. By the summer of 1863, southwestern Minnesota was emptied of nearly all the Native people who had lived there just one year prior.

Along with elements of land, profit, and politics, the fundamental component of race cannot be ignored. There is no doubt that racism and prejudice were prevalent throughout all of Minnesota in 1862. Even as Minnesotans sent soldiers to help the Union Army fight to end slavery, they called for racial extermination at home. Many historians have emphasized the role of the federal government in the removals of Indigenous nations across the Midwest. But the average citizens and European immigrants who settled the American West often organized, petitioned, and pushed the federal government into the hasty removals that cost many lives.

The culpability of regular men and women in ethnic cleansing events is just as great as that of the government. One scholar of Nazi Germany has found that even the most notorious genocide in history was carried out by "ordinary men" who were not necessarily antisemitic, nor were they even Nazi sympathizers, and they did not generally support Hitler. Christopher Browning's study of German Police Battalion 101 showed that the average men who perpetrated atrocities against Jews during the Holocaust were driven by what amounted to peer pressure, wartime fear, and dehumanization of the victims. In the same way, the Knights of the Forest took an oath to "prevail on others" to advocate their cause. In the ethnic cleansing of Minnesota, the citizenry exerted every pressure possible to force the federal government toward that end.[3]

Mankato elites also used racial imagery to justify and enlist support from settler-colonists and the federal government for their own political and economic goals. However, settler-colonists who felt they had lost land to the Ho-Chunk, experienced a brutal war with Dakota, and saw Native people in general as an annoyance and a threat did not need much prodding toward racial hatred. The reality of Blue Earth County in 1862 and 1863 was that political elites either projected an anti-Indian stance or they would no longer be politicians. The federal government had nothing to gain from Ho-Chunk removal aside from appeasing the settler-colonists, but the war and subsequent removal brought profits to Mankato businessmen. With the Civil War in full swing at the time, the federal government likely viewed the Ho-Chunk in Minnesota as a problem that should be dealt with and forgotten as quickly as possible. Minnesotans felt vehemently the same way.

In the end, it was both the settler-colonists and the Mankato business class that benefited from the removal of the Ho-Chunk. Within days of the Ho-Chunks' departure, settler-colonists had moved on to the reservation land, occupying houses and taking possession of already-planted fields so they could preempt claims. The government sold the Blue Earth reservation lands through a bidding process. Buyers included eastern land speculators and Minnesota elites, who resold the lands to farmers and preemptors for a hefty return. Chapman, Meagher, and the Barney brothers all purchased land, along with many petition signers, including Senator Morton Wilkinson. Alexander Ramsey even made claims for land on behalf of the state. It is probable that most Knights of the Forest members profited in some way or another from the removal of the Ho-Chunk from Minnesota. Asa Barney's older brother, with whom he shared several business ventures, was said to have closed an existing business because he made "more money in Winnebago lands." Charles A. Chapman was quite likely correct when he suggested that the prosperity of the white settler-colonists in the county was owed to the Knights and the removal of the Ho-Chunk. The entire region benefited economically from the profits made off the sale of Ho-Chunk reservation lands in Blue Earth County.[4]

Although there has been movement toward US-Dakota War reconciliation and commemoration in Mankato, the history of Ho-Chunk people in Blue Earth County is rarely acknowledged. In a ceremony held at Reconciliation Park in Mankato to commemorate the 150th anniversary of the Dakota hangings, the city added an installation that displayed the names of the thirty-eight executed Dakota men. Today, many Mankatoans make an extra effort to recognize the town's wrongdoings during the US-Dakota War. Every year, people gather at Reconciliation Park for ceremonies that feature Dakota speakers and acknowledge the imprisonment and the hangings.

Meanwhile, there has been only one relatively low-key public reconciliation program for Ho-Chunk people in Blue Earth County, organized in 2005 by longtime Mankato reconciliation advocates Bruce and Sheryl Dowlin and a few other local people. And there is no mention anywhere in the park of the Ho-Chunk people who lived there peacefully and were hunted by a secret society of Mankato founders.[5]

The issue here is not to question who suffered the greater injustice or who deserves the greater acknowledgment. It is more an issue of recognizing history. In the afterword for *Spaces of Hate*, Daniel M. Welliver writes, "Communities have histories of hate, i.e., their own unique organizational institutions, seminal events, and ingrained attitudes and patterns of behavior." For Mankatoans and Minnesotans to take a complete and honest look at their distinctive history of relations with Indigenous people, the Knights of the Forest must be recognized along with the hangings in histories of the US-Dakota War.[6]

This failure of historical memory is somewhat odd. In 1862, the Dakota people lived sixty miles from Mankato, in another county. The Ho-Chunk were a part of everyday life in the town. Mankato newspapers often discussed the Ho-Chunk people, their traders who were part of the business community, and the likelihood or timing of a reservation removal. Blue Earth County residents did not seem very concerned with Dakota people until hostilities commenced. When the war had begun, Mankatoans feared they were in a "precarious situation," sandwiched between the Ho-Chunk and Dakota reservations. Mankato newspapers covered the battles but also maintained a focus on the Ho-Chunk, asking whether they would join the Dakota and if the Ho-Chunk would finally be removed as news organizations and leaders had advocated for years.[7]

It is understandable that Mankatoans view the largest mass hanging in US history as their wartime legacy, but it is an incomplete historical image. The Ho-Chunk people were victims of Mankato profiteers' prosperity and "progress" before and after the war. Some Knights of the Forest members lived comfortably in Mankato as lawyers, businessmen, and civic leaders for the rest of their lives. For many years after the war, members recognized each other via the group's secret grips, passwords, and hand signs. The Knights of the Forest "Ritual" document was literally built into the foundations of Mankato Normal School by the town's earliest leaders. For some, the unusually large mass hanging might have been the most memorable US–Dakota War moment. But in the shadow of that terrible event, the Knights of the Forest and the community that supported them perpetuated a deep devastation upon the Ho-Chunk.[8]

The Ho-Chunk have, of course, outlasted the Knights of the Forest. More than one thousand Ho-Chunk people live in

Spoon-de-Kaury, or Spoon Decorah, sat for a portrait in Madison, Wisconsin, in 1887. *Photo by Edward R. Curtiss, Wisconsin Historical Society, WHI-11242*

Minnesota today. They participate in Ho-Chunk Nation matters as residents of District 4–the designation for tribal members living outside of Wisconsin.

They are part of a larger story of survival. The Ho-Chunk resisted decades of attempted ethnic cleansing in present-day Wisconsin and Illinois. In 1874, the US government finally stopped trying to evict the Ho-Chunk people from Wisconsin, and the Ho-Chunk began buying back land in their homeland from those who had taken it. The Ho-Chunk Nation of Wisconsin, a federally recognized tribal nation without a reservation, is now headquartered in Black River Falls, Wisconsin. It maintains a branch office in St. Paul and owns trust lands in Minnesota, within Houston County near La Crescent. The Winnebago Reservation in northeastern Nebraska is the home of the federally recognized Winnebago Tribe of Nebraska.

In Minnesota, there are eleven formally recognized tribal nations–seven Ojibwe and four Dakota. The Ho-Chunk are not among them. Though Minnesota organizations and institutions sometimes include the Ho-Chunk in land acknowledgments, Minnesota's state, county, and local governments– and its general public–do not understand or acknowledge the claims of the Ho-Chunk to their ancestral homelands within the state. Because the 1825 Treaty of Prairie du Chien abolished the Ho-Chunk people's tie to the parts of their traditional homelands in what became Minnesota, because actions of the US government forced the Ho-Chunk people to move *five times in twenty-five years*, and because their Minnesota reservations were abolished and their lands taken by settler-colonists, the Ho-Chunk are rarely remembered as part of the state's history or named among Minnesota's Indigenous groups.

The experience of the Ho-Chunk people in Minnesota during the nineteenth century illuminates the devastation heaped on their descendants, who have persevered and now continue their work for language and cultural renewal. The magnitude of this shameful treatment may help explain the levels of unacknowledged anti-Indian racism and denial in Minnesota. But knowing the truth behind hard histories can help us recognize their legacies of harm. If white Minnesotans can engage in this kind of truth telling more often, hate groups who think like the Knights of the Forest could be forever banished. And the Ho-Chunk people's persistence is an example to every group resisting such powerful forces. The Ho-Chunk are still here.

Ho-Chunk artist Linda Lucero of Black River Falls, Wisconsin, beaded these Reebok baby shoes, about 1990. *Wisconsin Historical Society, WHI-160424*

ACKNOWLEDGMENTS

I would like to thank the Ho-Chunk people who took the time to read, discuss, and share the draft manuscript, as well as those who emailed, called, answered questions, and connected me with others to help me better and more accurately understand and present their history. My friend Robert Pilot was especially helpful in all these regards as well as giving me a good understanding of the current standing of Ho-Chunk people in Minnesota. This book is intended to support the start of justice and reconciliation work for them by publicly acknowledging what Ho-Chunk people experienced in 1862–63.

I also thank the staff at Mankato State University Archives, Blue Earth County Historical Society, and the Minnesota Historical Society Gale Family Library for providing most of the primary source material for this book. Their services were crucial to my research during a global pandemic.

Many individuals supported this project. But no one matched the immense effort of Minnesota Historical Society Press editor in chief Ann Regan, who spent years working with me on the manuscript. I am grateful to her for the countless phone calls, emails, and suggestions that ensured this book is published at its best.

This book would not be the same without the skilled map-making of Cole Sutton. He undertook this project when I first started in graduate school and patiently saw it through to its publication as a book almost a decade later. His excellent work added a depth to this story that cannot be communicated with words.

I am also thankful to my colleagues and friends Tina Gross and Blair Tosh for their unwavering support and ready advice. The candid discussions between us over the years have shaped my thinking. Tina especially encouraged me to research and write about this topic when I first had the idea over a decade ago.

I'm fortunate to have a supportive family. My husband, Rob, and children, Jackson and Jenna, graciously volunteered as research assistants, searching for books, counting names on petitions, and organizing my files. Jackson and Jenna especially motivated me to do this work for the future of history. This research is just a starting point, and I know their generation will find new and better ways to tell these stories.

APPENDIX A

Senate and House of Representatives of the State of Minnesota, Joint Resolution Relative to the Sioux and Winnebago Reservations, 1858

Whereas, The reservation now occupied by the Sioux Indians, embraces a much larger tract of country than is necessary for their use, or computable with the interests of the State, and whereas, the civilization of these Indians would be greatly promoted by securing to each head of family a tract of land sufficient for agricultural purposes, with such assistance from the general government as may be deemed requisite to withdraw them from the chase and afford proper agricultural and mechanical education.

And, whereas. The reservation now occupied by the Winnebago Indians, in the counties of Blue Earth and Waseca, embraces a territory now entirely surrounded by white settlements, and which reservation is near the centre of one of the most densely populated districts of the State.

And, Whereas, the location of said reservation is such, that it is impossible to prevent a constant trade being carried on between the white settlers and the Indians occupying the said reserve, and through the influence constantly kept up between the whites and the Indians, the latter are constantly being supplied with spirituous liquors, the free use of which by the Indians often leads to the most unfortunate results, both as relates to the whites and the Indians. And whereas the civilization of these Indians would doubtless be greatly advanced by removing them beyond the influence above alluded to, and by locating them upon lands where each Indian can be possessed of a farm beyond the white settlements.

Therefore, Resolved by the Senate and House of Representatives of the State of Minnesota, that our Senators and Representatives in Congress, be and are hereby requested to urge upon the Indian department at Washington, such measures as may be necessary to open to settlement the surplus and unoccupied land now contained within the Sioux reservation, and such additional measures as may be deemed proper to heal the difficulties heretofore and still existing between the whites and Sioux, bordering upon our State line, and to secure the peaceful occupancy of the lands upon our western frontiers. And also to take such measures as may [be] necessary to procure a speedy removal of the said Winnebago Indians from their present location, to one beyond the white settlements, and that the reservation now occupied by the said Winnebago Indians may be opened to pre-emption and settlement in the same manner as other government lands are now subject to settlement.

GEORGE BRADLEY,
Speaker *pro tem.* of the House of Representatives.
RICHARD G. MURPHY,
President *pro tem.* of the Senate.
APPROVED—February twenty-fifth, one thousand eight hundred and fifty-eight.
CHARLES L. CHASE, Acting Governor;
SECRETARY'S OFFICE, Minnesota, ⎫
February 25, 1858. ⎭
I hereby certify the foregoing to be a true copy of the original on file in this office.
CHAS. L. CHASE, Secretary.

APPENDIX B

"The Knights of the Forest: A Secret History," *Mankato Review*, April 27, 1886

(Written for the REVIEW.)

No event in the history of Minnesota caused more universal anxiety and alarm in the minds of its citizens, than the Sioux massacre of 1862. Mankato was then a frontier town. The whole country west of us had been devastated by the bloodthirsty Indians, about a thousand of our people murdered by these savages; their houses and crops destroyed; our town converted into a camp of fugitives, and a hospital for wounded men, women and children. It is no wonder that a bitter mid revengeful feeling prevailed among the white settlers.

Added to all this, there was a general feeling of insecurity, arising from the fact that only three miles from Mankato lay the Winnebago Indian reservation, on which this tribe had a few years before been placed by the United States government, occupying nine townships of the most fertile and best watered portion of Blue Earth and Waseca counties.

The white settlers on this track had been driven from their homes to make room for the Indians. Some of them who tried to hold their claims were subjected to constant threats, annoyances, and depredations by the savages until they, too, unable to exist longer in such continual fear, abandoned their homes, and the land which they had hoped soon to behold occupied by a prosperous community, was forced by process of law to remain a wilderness.

These Winnebagoes [sic] were known to be friendly with the Sioux, and only the most watchful care and vigilance had prevented them from joining in the murderous raid. Our people felt that the future prosperity of Mankato, and indeed of all this region, depended on obtaining the speedy removal of the Winnebagoes from our vicinity, and even from our State. It was, however, a difficult project owing to the great influence with the government of those whose interest it was to have them remain, and the case seemed almost hopeless.

While affairs were in this condition, the date being the last of December, 1862, or the first of January 1863, three persons, two of them citizens of Mankato, and one of Garden City, conversing about the situation, conceived the idea of forming a secret order, whose object should be the removal of all Indians from the State. Having confided the project to others, chosen men, believed to be favorable, and found to be so, they organized a lodge that very night, in a building in block 14, opposite the levee, and adopted the name, "Knights of the Forest." They believed that by uniting men of both political parties to work for a common object throwing over their proceedings the mysterious veil of secrecy, they would be able to wield more power than by working openly by petitions or otherwise.

This lodge afterwards met in a carpenter's shop that stood on the corner of Front and Jackson streets, where the *Free Press* office now stands. Then in an office in block 14 again, near Walnut street. Then a few times in the Masonic Hall, in Marks' stone building, and probably in other places. They considered it expedient to move from place to place, lest they might attract attention by meeting many times in one building.

The lodge grew to a considerable size. It included in its membership many of the most prominent and influential men of Mankato and Blue Earth county, some of whom still live among us, and have not forgotten the ancient grip and sign, which have frequently, even in these latter years, afforded a means of recognition between men who would otherwise have regarded each other as strangers. A ritual was adopted. the presiding officer was called Worthy Chancellor, other officers were Past Chancellor, Vice Chancellor, Conductor, Assistant Conductor, recording and Financial Secretaries and Sentinel. At the opening of the lodge, the Chancellor addressed the members as follows:

"OFFICERS AND MEMBERS: — The objects for which we are assembled are worthy of our cause. It is no less than the preservation of our lives, our families and our homes. Let us be ever, watchful and keep constantly in mind the sacred obligation which binds us together as brothers in one common interest. I sincerely hope that this meeting may be profitable to each one of us, and that we may go forth from this lodge stronger and braver in the determination to banish forever from our beautiful State every Indian who now desecrates its soil."

The Vice Chancellor then proclaimed the lodge open in the following words: "I declare this lodge open for the transaction of business, [and] for extending universal opposition to all tribes of Indians in the state of Minnesota."

At the initiation the candidate was asked the following questions before he was admitted to the lodge room:

Do you promise, upon your honor, that you will keep all secrets and information which we may here reveal to you? Are you in favor of the removal of all tribes of Indians from the State of Minnesota? Will you sacrifice all political and other preferences to accomplish that object? Will you do all in your power to elect to office such men only as will favor such removal? Do you desire to become a member of an order having for its object the removal of all Indians from this State, called the Knights of the Forest?"

These questions having been satisfactorily answered, he was led by the conductor within the lodge room, and introduced to the Vice Chancellor, who addressed him, explaining the objects of the order. After this the candidate took the obligation, which was as follows:

"I, _____, of my own free will and accord, in the full belief that every Indian should be removed from the State, by the memory of the inhuman cruelties perpetrated upon defenceless [sic] citizens, and in the presence of the members of the order here assembled, do most solemnly promise, without any mental reservation whatever, to use every exertion and influence in my power, to cause the removal of all tribes of Indians from the State of Minnesota. I will sacrifice every political and other preference to accomplish that object. I will not aid or assist in any manner to elect to office in this State or the United States any person outside of this order who will not publicly or privately pledge himself for the permanent removal of all tribes of Indians from the State of Minnesota. I will protect and defend at every hazard, all members in carrying out the objects of this order. I will faithfully observe the constitution, rules and by-laws of this lodge or any grand or working lodge of Knights of the Forest to which I may be attached. I will never in any manner reveal the name, existence or secrets of this order to any person not entitled to know the same. And in case I should be expelled or voluntarily withdraw from the order, I will consider this obligation still binding. To all of which I pledge my sacred honor.

After receiving this obligation the candidate was required to sign the constitution, and was then instructed in the grip, sign and password, after which the Past Worthy Chancellor addressed him with congratulatory remarks, and finally the Chancellor proclaimed him a worthy knight, entitled to all the rights of the order.

When the lodge had increased to a considerable size, having in its membership not only many citizens of Mankato, but also several from the surrounding country, applications began to come for the forming of other lodges. A grand lodge was therefore organized, with headquarters at Mankato, which proceeded to grant charters to subordinate lodges, several of which were formed in the winter and spring of 1863; one at Garden City, which met in the garret of an unoccupied house; one at Meriden, Steele county, and others, the names and locations of which are now lost, the records of the grand lodge and of Mankato lodge having been destroyed by fire.

The nature of the business transacted in these lodges will be readily understood from a perusal of the obligation recited above. One noteworthy act of the Mankato lodge, however, merits particular attention. This was the employment of a certain number of men, members of the order, whose duty was to lie in ambush on the outskirts of the Winnebago Reservation, and shoot any Indian who might be observed outside the lines. It is not the province of this sketch to relate how many, if any, Indians were thus disposed of. It is sufficient to say that the designated parties went out on their scouting excursions, and in due time returned and reported. For obvious reasons their reports were not made matter of record.

The Winnebagos were removed in May 1863, and with their removal, and the opening of the reservation for settlement, the immediate reason for the organization of the Knights of the Forest ceased to exist. The order, however, had done its work. There is no doubt that its prestige was magnified in the minds of the people, and of the government, by the secrecy thrown around its proceedings. This mystery had its effect on the government, and it is very probable that without the removal of the Indians might have been delayed for years, as there was a strong and influential party whose interest it was to have them remain.

There is no betrayal of trust in publishing these matters, now since the object for which the order was constituted having been accomplished, and the order itself having ceased forever, the people are now among those who, in the language of the ritual, are "entitled to know the same."

Those who carefully read the obligation may wonder how new members were obtained, since the obligation prohibited revealing the name or existence of the order. It was the practice to approach those who were believed to be in sympathy with the project of removing the Indians, and talk with them in a casual manner on this subject, and finally, unless they themselves suggested it, ask them what they thought of the propriety of forming such an order. If the result of the interview was favorable, a report was then made to the lodge; it was talked over, and if, a ballot being had, the person was elected, he was then requested confidentially to come to a certain place at a certain time, where he would meet others who were ready to join him. On arriving at the designated place, and not before, he discovered that the lodge was already in existence.

APPENDIX C

"Ritual," The Initiation Rites and Oath of the Knights of the Forest

OPENING.

[When the hour arrives for opening the Lodge, the Worthy Chancellor (and in his absence the Worthy Vice Chancellor) will take the chair and call the Lodge to order by giving one rap.]

Worthy Chancellor. The officers will take their stations. The Conductor will see that the Lodge is guarded in a proper manner. The Conductor will examine those present, that all may be worthy.

[If any are present, without the pass word, they must leave the room.]

C. [Reports to W. C.]

W. C. [The chancellor gives three raps, all the members rise.]

Officers and members: The objects for which we are assembled, are worthy of our cause. It is no less than the preservation of our lives, our families, and our homes. Let us be ever watchful and keep constantly in mind the sacred obligation which binds us together as brothers in one common interest. I sincerely hope this meeting may be profitable to each one of

[us], and that we may go forth from this Lodge stronger and braver in the determination to banish forever from our beautiful State every Indian who now desecrates our soil.

W. C. The Worthy Vice Chancellor will now open this Lodge.

W. V. C. By direction of our worthy Chancellor, I declare this Lodge open for the transaction of business and for extending universal opposition to all tribes of Indians in the State of Minnesota.

[The W. C. gives one rap and the members take their seats.]

W. C. The Financial secretary will call the roll of members.

INITIATION.

[When the Lodge is ready for initiation the F. S. will retire with the Assistant Conductor, to collect the initiation fees when the A. C. shall propound to the candidate following questions:]

C. Before you can proceed any further, you must give your assent to the following questions.

Question. Do you promise upon your honor that you will keep all secrets and information which I may here reveal to you?

Answer. I do.

Question. Are you in favor of the removal of all tribes of Indians from the State of Minnesota?

Answer. I am.

Question. Will you sacrifice all political and other preferences to accomplish that object?

Answer. I will.

Question. Will you do all in your power to elect to office such men only as will favor such removal?

Answer. I will.

Question. Do you desire to become a member of an order

having for its object the removal of all Indians from this State, called the Knights of the Forest?

Answer. I do.

[The F. S. collects his fee, and the questions having been answered in the affirmative the officers return to the Lodge room and report.]

F. S. All correct, Worthy Chancellor.

C. The usual questions are answered the affirmative, Worthy Chancellor.

W. C. The Conductor will introduce the candidate.

[The Conductor, taking the candidate by his arm and leading him to the door, gives three raps. The Conductor introduces the candidate to the Worthy Vice Chancellor.]

C. Worthy Vice Chancellor, permit to introduce our friend, who wishes to become a member of our order.

W. V. C. My friend: It is with the utmost gratification that we proceed to comply with your wishes. None but those whose honor and integrity are unquestioned, can enter our circle. We have full faith in your integrity. We place implicit confidence in you, that you will never betray the secrets of our order. The atrocious murders visited upon innocent, honest and industrious citizens has proved to us, that our only security is in mutual protection and united action. We have learned, at the cost of many lives, that the white man and the Indian cannot dwell together in peace and harmony. The chief object of this order is to prevent the permanent location of any tribe of Indians in this State. The field open before us is wide and our success will depend in a great measure upon our energy. You have chosen the only path which will give security and safety to the future, and prevent the blow of the glittering knife and merciless tomahawk. In becoming a member of this order you will be required to bind yourself to its laws by a solemn obligation—an obligation which will in nowise transcend that inherent right implanted in our natures by a wise Creator. "The right of self-preservation." With these assurances and this warning, we now proceed to inform you further in relation to the duties of our order.

W. V. C. Conductor, take charge of our friend and present him to the Worthy Chancellor for obligation and instruction.

C. Worthy Chancellor, I here present our friend for obligation.

W.C. My friend, before you can become a worthy member of our fraternity, you must give your free and cordial assent to a solemn and binding obligation. That obligation requires that you should use all your influence and power for the removal of all tribes of Indians from the State of Minnesota. We deem it in accordance with the duty which every citizen owes to himself, his neighbors and his country.

OBLIGATION.

I, _____, of my own free will and accord, in the full belief that every Indian should be removed from the State, by the memory of the inhuman cruelties perpetrated upon defenseless citizens, and in the presence of the members of this order here assembled, do most solemnly promise, without any mental reservation whatever, to use every exertion and influence in my power to cause the removal of all tribes of Indians from the State of Minnesota. I will sacrifice every political and other preference to accomplish that object. I will not aid or assist in any manner to elect to office in this State or the United States any person outside of this order, who will not publicly or privately pledge himself for the permanent removal of all Indians from the State of Minnesota. I will protect and defend, at every hazzard, all members in carrying out the objectives of this order. I will faithfully observe the constitution, rules and by-laws of this Lodge or any Grand or working lodge of Knights of the Forest to which I may be attached. I will never in any manner reveal the name, existence, or secrets of this order to any person not entitle[d] to know the same; and in case I should be expelled or voluntarily withdraw from this order, I will consider this obligation still binding. To this I pledge my sacred honor.

The candidate will now sign our constitution and obligation.

W. C. You will now sign our constitution, after which you will be further instructed.

W. C. I will now instruct you in the signs, pass words, grips, and tokens of this order.

1st. I will first instruct you in the signs of recognition and the test word.

2d. The pass-word is to be given only by the Worthy Chancellor in the Lodge room.

3d. The Conductor will now instruct you in the grip.

4th. I will now inform you how to work your way into or out of this or any other Lodge.

I have some further instructions to give you in reference to the acquiring of members to our order.

The P. W. will instruct the candidates upon the constitution in reference to admission of members.

C. Past Worthy Chancellor, I am directed by the Worthy Chancellor to present this friend to be further instructed in the duties of this order.

P. W. C. I extend to you our heartfelt congratulations on the progress you have made thus far in the order of the Knights of the Forest. You are bound by every honorable motive to consider yourself in such a manner as never to bring reproach upon our order. You will ever keep in mind your sacred obligation, and you will remember that one of the great duties of your life is not only to advocate the banishment of all Indians from this State, but to prevail on others to do so. Every influence in your power should be given to this one great object;

and when this accursed race of infuriated demons shall be driven far away towards the setting sun—when these beautiful prairies which are now homeless and destitute shall again bloom into a paradise of industry and wealth—you will have cause to rejoice that you were ever a member of this order.

W. C. The Worthy Vice Chancellor will now make the proclamation.

W. V. C. Worthy associates, our Chancellor is about to proclaim this person a worthy knight. Is such your will and pleasure?

All respond: It is.

W. C. Then in the name of the Grand Lodge of the Knights of the Forest I proclaim this person a worthy knight and he is entitled to all the rights guaranteed by our Constitution and by-laws. Trusting you may become a worthy knight of our fraternity, I now welcome you to our circle.

ORDER OF BUSINESS.

1. Reading minutes of previous meeting.
2. Reception [of] communications.
3. Reports of permanent committee on candidates.
4. Balloting for candidates.
5. Initiation of candidates.
6. Proposals for membership.
7. Reports of special committees.
8. Unfinished business.
9. Advancement of the order.

APPENDIX D

"Removal of the Winnebago Indians," Petition to the President of the United States and to the Secretary of the Interior, January 21, 1863

To the President of the United States and to the Secretary of the Interior—The undersigned, citizens of the State of Minnesota and residents of the county immediately adjacent to the Winnebago Reservation, respectfully represent and petition:

That the terrible events which have just transpired in this neighborhood clearly prove "that the rich, productive counties surrounding the reservation must be vacated, and the pleasant homes which have cost so much privation and sacrifice, must be given up by those who now possess them, or the Indians must vacate their reservation. These people cannot longer remain in close proximity. The reason is apparent. These Indians are now located upon a small reservations [*sic*], about eighteen miles in length by nine in breadth; there is but little game upon this tract, and by the terms of the treaty they must remain upon it. The annuity of these Indians, although considerable, is not sufficient to keep them from starvation. Their idle, dissolute habits prevent their performing any useful labor, and hence, for years, they have been in the habit of wandering over the adjacent country, plundering the occupants of the ceded territory, and committing depredations upon the people wherever they went. With a marvelous patience the people have for years submitted to their annoyance, and perhaps they might have longer remained quiet but for the horrid massacre in their midst, which, from its sudden violence and brutality shocked and alarmed the people of the entire State. Henceforth the Indians cannot be permitted to leave their reservation, and to be confined to it is starvation, for they will not work. Hence the removal of the Indians is a necessity. Humanity requires it; the welfare of the Indians, as well as the peace of the whites demand it." *Letter of Hon. J. S. Wilkinson to Judge Cleveland.*

We therefore most respectfully ask that the Winnebago tribe of Indians be immediately removed beyond the borders of our state.

NOTES

Notes to Chapter 1: Hidden History Preserved

1. *Mankato Weekly Record*, June 26, 1869; Jarvis, *Time Capsules*, 10, 102; *St. Cloud Times*, October 7, 1992; "Time Capsules," Minnesota Historical Society, https://mnhs.gitlab.io/archive/conservation /www.mnhs.org/preserve/conservation/timecapsule.html; *Litchfield Independent Review*, September 6, 2015.

2. *College Reporter*, May 7, September 30, 1968; Old Main Cornerstone Collection finding aid, University Archives, Minnesota State University, Mankato, https://archivesspace.lib.mnsu.edu/public /repositories/3/resources/370. The contents were published online as part of a graduate student project.

The term *US–Dakota War* is used here because the Dakota likely did declare war: see Routel, "Minnesota Bounties on Dakota Men during the US-Dakota War," 8n46, 60-68. For further understanding of the use of the term *American*, see Chomsky, "The United States-Dakota War Trials," 16n7. "US-Dakota War" is also the term used by a Dakota historian: see Waziyatawin, *What Does Justice Look Like?*, 38. On Knights groups in surrounding communities, see Hughes, *History of Blue Earth County*, 138.

"Ritual/Initiation, Grand Lodge of the Knights of the Forest," Old Main Cornerstone Collection, 1869-1969, Minnesota State University, Mankato.

This book uses the people's traditional name, Ho-Chunk. However, the name Winnebago is used when citing and quoting from government publications, newspapers, and other documents of this time, and in referring to place names like the Winnebago Agency. On the meaning of the names, see chapter 2.

3. *Mankato Review*, April 27, 1886, January 20, 1897; *Mankato Daily Review*, April 18, 1916; *Mankato Free Press*, January 15, 1929; *Mankato Daily Free Press*, May 4, 1926.

4. The terms *ethnic cleansing* and *genocide* both apply to the colonization of the United States as outlined by the United Nations' definitions for each, whereby "ethnic cleansing" is the process of forcibly moving people and "genocide" is the act of intentional attempts to destroy members of a nation or an ethnic, racial, or religious group: United Nations Commission of Experts, https://www.un.org/en/genocideprevention/ethnic-cleansing.shtml; United Nations Convention on the Prevention and Punishment of the Crime of Genocide, https://www.un.org/en/genocideprevention/genocide.shtml. For an understanding on the application of these terms to the colonization of North America, see Ostler, "Appendix 1. The Question of Genocide in U.S. History," *Surviving Genocide*, 383–87.

Anderson, *Conquest of Texas*; Lause, *Secret Society History of the Civil War*. Gary Clayton Anderson defines American settler colonization as ethnic cleansing rather than genocide, arguing that the Texas Rangers were not intent on extermination. This, however, ignores the fact that it meets the United Nations definitions of both. Although Mark Lause's work does not directly focus on atrocities committed by secret societies, he does describe the organizational social networks behind those described in Anderson's Texas book.

For an understanding of the US–Dakota War, see Anderson and Woolworth, eds., *Through Dakota Eyes*; Canku and Simon, *The Dakota Prisoner of War Letters*; Hyman, *Dakota Women's Work*; Waziyatawin, *What Does Justice Look Like?*; and Wingerd, *North Country*.

5. Hughes, *History of Blue Earth County*, 59–60, 99.

6. Bachman, "Colonel Miller's War."

Notes to Chapter 2: The People of the Big Voice

1. Lonetree, "Visualizing Native Survivance," 15; Kantrowitz, *Citizens of a Stolen Land*; Loew, *Indian Nations of Wisconsin*, 6, 44.

2. Richards, "Winnebago Subsistence"; Lurie, *Wisconsin Indians*, 6, 13–14.

3. Loew, *Indian Nations of Wisconsin*, 44-45; McBride, *Women's Wisconsin*, 3-5; Louise P. Kellogg, "Glory of the Morning and Decorah Family," *Madison Democrat*, February 12, 1912.

4. Murphy, "Autonomy and the Economic Roles of Indian Women," 81-82; Murphy, "Their Women Quite Industrious Miners," 36-53.

5. Murphy, "Autonomy and the Economic Roles of Indian Women," 81-82; Murphy, "Their Women Quite Industrious Miners"; Richards, "Winnebago Subsistence," 3-5; Hixson, "Adaptation, Resistance and Representation in the Modern US Settler State."

6. Loew, *Indian Nations of Wisconsin*, 46-47. Tecumseh's War ended decades of struggle for control of the Great Lakes region between the United States and various tribal nations. After Tecumseh and the American Indian Confederacy lost the Battle of Tippecanoe in 1811, many Indigenous people simply joined the British and continued to fight the United States in the War of 1812. Hall, *Uncommon Defense*, 80; Zanger, "Red Bird," 41-43; *Treaties between the Winnebago Indians and the United States of America, 1817-1856*.

7. "Ratified treaty no. 139, Documents relating to the negotiation of the treaty of August 19, 1825, with the Sioux, Chippewa, Sauk and Fox, Menominee, Iowa and Winnebago Indians and part of the Ottawa, and Potawatomi of the Illinois Indians," 28, http://digital.library.wisc.edu/1711.dl/History.IT1825no139; Mary A. Hunt to Joseph Blackwood, October 3, 1861. She claimed her father-in-law lived near the Ho-Chunk on the Mississippi River in 1812 and purchased land there from the Ho-Chunk in 1829: US Office of Indian Affairs, Letters Received by the Office of Indian Affairs, 1824-1880, Winnebago Agency, 1826-1875, reel 935 (hereafter Letters Received, Winnebago Agency). Spector, "Winnebago Indians," 44-46; Smith, "Ho-Chunk Tribal History," 5; Radin, *The Winnebago Tribe*, 3; Kantrowitz, *Citizens of a Stolen Land*, 25-26.

8. Zanger, "Red Bird," 67-69.

9. Hall, *Uncommon Defense*, 80; Zanger, "Red Bird," 64-87.

10. Shrake, "Chasing an Elusive War," 33-45.

11. "Ratified Treaty No. 148, Documents Relating to the Negotiation of the Treaty of August 11, 1827, with the Chippewa, Menominee and Winnebago Indians, August 11, 1827," 25-26, 31, 33, https://digital.library.wisc.edu/1711.dl/GYTF7SY2OLMED8E.

12. "Ratified Treaty No. 148," 18.

13. Zanger, "Red Bird," 77–78; Lonetree, "Visualizing Native Survivance," 16.

14. Rayman, "Confrontation at the Fever River Lead Mining District"; Case, *Relentless Business of Treaties*, 74–75, 79.

15. "Ratified Treaty No. 153, Documents Relating to the Negotiation of the Treaty of August 25, 1828, with the Winnebago and United Potawatomi, Chippewa, and Ottawa Indians," 9, https://digital.library.wisc.edu/1711.dl/GPHA2TBN7B5UN8X.

Notes to Chapter 3:
The Takeover of Ho-Chunk Homelands

1. "Ratified Treaty No. 153," 6, 13.

2. "Ratified Treaty No. 153," 18, 20; Lonetree, "Visualizing Native Survivance," 16.

3. Hall, *Uncommon Defense*, 9, 204, 211–13; "Ratified Treaty No. 310, Documents Relating to the Negotiation of the Treaty of April 15, 1859, with the Winnebago Indians," https://digital.library.wisc.edu/1711.dl/XMIPADJKPD4AV8C.

4. Lonetree, "Visualizing Native Survivance," 17; Harstad, "Disease and Sickness on the Wisconsin Frontier," 254; Smith, "Ho-Chunk Tribal History," 54.

5. Lonetree, "Visualizing Native Survivance," 17; Diedrich, *Winnebago Oratory*, 58.

6. Hall, *Uncommon Defense*, 260–61.

7. Bieder, *Native American Communities in Wisconsin*, 171. Letters Received, Winnebago Agency, reels 931–946, includes numerous letters and petitions sent by people in Wisconsin, including the governor, over sixty-six years, asking for federal authorities to remove the Ho-Chunk.

8. De La Ronde, "Personal Narrative," 364–65.

9. Lurie, "The Winnebago Indians," 170–71.

10. Pluth, "Account of Winnebago Affairs at Long Prairie," 6–7.

Notes to Chapter 4:
Ho-Chunk Removals in Minnesota Territory

1. Wingerd, *North Country*, 136–37; Pluth, "Failed Watab Treaty," 4–5.
2. See Wingerd, *North Country*.
3. Pluth, "Account of Winnebago Affairs at Long Prairie."
4. Case, *Relentless Business of Treaties*, 39, 60–61, 91.
5. Pluth, "Failed Watab Treaty," 5–7.
6. Orlando Brown to Alexander Ramsey, April 15, 1850; Henry H. Sibley to Orlando Brown, April 18, 1850; Orlando Brown to Henry H. Sibley, April 25, 1850; and Master Roll of Winnebago Indians Removed by Henry M. Rice from May 2, 1850, to June 20, 1850—all in Letters Received, Winnebago Agency, reels 932–933; Folwell, *History of Minnesota*, 1: 313–18; Jorstad, "Personal Politics in the Origin of Minnesota's Democratic Party," 267.
7. Wingerd, *North Country*, 222.
8. Pluth, "Failed Watab Treaty," 13–18.
9. Pluth, "Failed Watab Treaty," 18.

Notes to Chapter 5:
The Theft of Minnesota and the Call for Extermination

1. For an understanding of early Minnesota history and the Dakota treaties, see Westerman and White, *Mni Sota Makoce*; Anderson, *Little Crow*; and Wingerd, *North Country*. Westerman and White, *Mni Sota Makoce*, 173–79, provides side-by-side comparisons of the 1851 Treaty of Traverse des Sioux in English, in the Dakota version read aloud at the time, and in a modern re-translation of that Dakota version.
2. Westerman and White, *Mni Sota Makoce*.
3. Anderson, *Little Crow*, 82, 121, 130; Pluth, "Failed Watab Treaty," 17–18.
4. Hughes, *History of Blue Earth County*, 59–60. Waseca County, incorporating part of Blue Earth County, was created in 1857.
5. Chatelain, "Federal Land Policy and Minnesota Politics," 237; Hughes, *History of Blue Earth County*, 60–70; "Pre-emptors on Home Reservation of Winnebago Indians, Letter from the Secretary of

the Interior," Congressional Serial Set, issue 1189, vol. 9, ex. doc. 50, March 9, 1864.

6. Katrowitz, *Citizens of a Stolen Land*, 87, 89; "Ratified Treaty No. 310," 19; Edward Wolcott to William P. Dole, August 1, 1861, Letters Received, Winnebago Agency, reel 935.

7. Hughes, *History of Blue Earth County*, 237, 99.

8. Kappler, ed., *Indian Affairs: Laws and Treaties. Vol. II (Treaties)*, 790–92; Wolcott to Dole, August 1, 1861; Katrowitz, *Citizens of a Stolen Land*, 87–89.

9. Agent Balcombe to William P. Dole, Letters Received, Winnebago Agency, reel 935; Lass, "Ginseng Rush in Minnesota," 260. Ginseng was used as a tonic; see Peterson and LaBatte, *Voices from Pejuhutazizi*, where the authors note that ginseng was also used for men's sexual health.

10. Hughes, *History of Blue Earth County*, 59.

11. White, "The Power of Whiteness"; Hughes, *History of Blue Earth County*, 59.

12. Hughes, *History of Blue Earth County*, 63; Chapman, *History of Mankato Lodge No. 12*; Chapman, *Mankato and Blue Earth County*; Griswold, *Mankato and Blue Earth County*; Willard, *Blue Earth County*.

13. Hughes, *History of Blue Earth County*, 60, 68.

14. Hughes, *History of Blue Earth County*, 64; White, "Indian Visits."

15. Minnesota Legislature, *Joint Resolution Relative to the Sioux and Winnebago Reservations. February 25, 1858*.

16. Sorensen, "Press Coverage of the Dakota Conflict of 1862," 101, 106.

17. For a good understanding of the US–Dakota Conflict of 1862, here and in the following paragraphs, see Wingerd, *North Country*, and Anderson, *Massacre in Minnesota*. On Myrick's insult, see Hubbard and Holcombe, *Minnesota in Three Centuries*, 3:286, 396.

18. *Report of the Commissioner of Indian Affairs for the Year 1862*, 237.

19. *Message of Governor Ramsey to the Legislature of Minnesota, Delivered September 9, 1862*, 12; Quaife, "The Panic of 1862 in Wisconsin"; *Report of the Commissioner of Indian Affairs for the Year 1862*, 237; Edward Salomon to John Palmer Usher, July 2, 10, 21, 28, 1863 – all from Letters Received, Winnebago Agency, reel 936.

20. *Mankato Weekly Review*, April 6, 13, 20, 27, and May 4, 11, 1897.

21. Monjeau-Marz, *Dakota Indian Internment at Fort Snelling*.

22. Bachman, "Colonel Miller's War"; *Mankato Semi-Weekly Record*, December 6, 1862; Bachman, *Northern Slave, Black Dakota*, 243–45.

23. Bachman, "Colonel Miller's War," 109, 113–16.

24. Alexander Ramsey, *Proclamation to the People of Minnesota*, December 6, 1862.

Notes to Chapter 6: Mankato Men and the Secret Society Tradition

1. On the hanging, see Wingerd, *North Country*, 324–28; Chomsky, "The United States–Dakota War Trials"; and Brown, *Bury My Heart at Wounded Knee*, 138–46; on the singing of the hymn, see Peterson and LaBatte, *Voices from Pejuhutazizi*, 93.

2. *Mankato Review*, April 27, 1886, January 20, 1897; *Mankato Daily Review*, April 18, 1916; *Mankato Free Press*, January 15, 1929.

3. Hughes, *History of Blue Earth County*, 361.

4. Hughes, *History of Blue Earth County*, 98, 362; Semicentennial Committee, *Mankato: Its First Fifty Years*, 193–94.

5. *Mankato Review*, April 27, 1886. Materials from this article appear verbatim in the signed article Chapman published in the *Mankato Daily Review*, April 18, 1916. Chapman, *History of Mankato Lodge No. 12*, 55–56.

6. *Mankato Review*, April 27, 1886; *Mankato Daily Review*, April 18, 1916 ("234 square miles"); Chapman, *History of Mankato Lodge No. 12*, 55–56; Chapman, *Mankato and Blue Earth County*.

7. Chapman, *History of Mankato Lodge No. 12*; Charles Chapman, journals, 1856–57, 1876, Blue Earth County Historical Society, Mankato; Chapman, *Mankato and Blue Earth County*, 8.

8. Hughes, *History of Blue Earth County*, 99, 237, 285.

9. Hughes, *History of Blue Earth County*, 92, 284–86; Semicentennial Committee, *Mankato: Its First Fifty Years*, 106; Minnesota Legislative Reference Library, "Porter, John J. 'J. J.', G. A.,'" http://www.leg.state.mn.us/legdb/fulldetail.aspx?id=14403; *Mankato Record*, October 4, 1862.

10. John J. Porter, 1857 Minnesota Territorial Census, Census ID

4231374, Blue Earth River, Blue Earth County, Minnesota, United States, Line 27; Hughes, *History of Blue Earth County*, 285.

11. Hughes, *History of Blue Earth County*, 113; *Mankato Free Press*, November 1, 1905; John J. Porter, 1857 Census ID 4231374; *Chicago Daily Tribune*, January 15, 1929.

12. E. D. B. Porter, 1875 Minnesota State Census, Census ID 4230520, Rose, Ramsey County, Minnesota, United States; *Mankato Free Press*, December 22, 1891; Chapman, *History of Mankato Lodge No. 12*, 35, 67; "Removal of the Winnebago Indians," petition, February 25, 1862, Letters Received, Winnebago Agency, reel 936 (see Appendix D in this book); Hughes, *History of Blue Earth County*, 125; Semi-centennial Committee, *Mankato: Its First Fifty Years*, 331–33; *Mankato Daily Free Press*, March 20, 1895.

13. Hughes, *History of Blue Earth County*, 116; *St. Paul Pioneer*, August 22, 1862; Minnesota Legislative Reference Library, "Porter, John J. 'J. J., G. A.'"; J. J. Porter, 1865 Minnesota State Census, Census ID 4231179, Mankato, Blue Earth County, Minnesota, United States, lines 12–18; Internal Revenue Assessment Lists for Minnesota, 1862–1866, Records of the Internal Revenue Service; *Grange Advance* (Red Wing, MN), March 11, 1874; *Mankato Record*, March 7, 1874; *Mankato Review*, March 13, 1874; *Mankato Union*, March 13, 1874.

14. *St. Paul Daily Globe*, November 7, 1879; John J. Porter, 1895 Minnesota State Census, Census ID 4231378, St. Paul, Ramsey County, Minnesota, United States, line 1–2; John Porter, 1905 Minnesota State Census, Census ID 4231339, St. Paul, Ramsey County, Minnesota, United States; *Irish Standard* (Minneapolis), August 2, 1913; *Chicago Daily Tribune*, January 15, 1929; *Mankato Daily Free Press*, March 26, 1895; Semi-centennial Committee, *Mankato: Its First Fifty Years*, 214–15; *Mankato Free Press*, January 14, 1929.

15. Hughes, *History of Blue Earth County*, 139; *Mankato Record*, May 2, 1863.

16. Hughes, *History of Blue Earth County*, 327–28; Semi-centennial Committee, *Mankato: Its First Fifty Years*, 172–75.

17. Old Settlers' Reunion Notes, Thomas Hughes Papers, Minnesota State University, Mankato.

18. Hughes, *History of Blue Earth County*, 138, 233, 327–28; Semi-centennial Committee, *Mankato: Its First Fifty Years*, 85, 172–75;

Mankato Review, April 27, 1886; Chapman, *History of Mankato Lodge No. 12*.

19. For further reading on fraternal organizations in the nineteenth century, see de la Cova, "Filibusters and Freemasons"; Keehn, Knights of the Golden Circle; Klement, *Dark Lanterns*; and Lause, *Secret Society History of the Civil War*.

20. Semi-centennial Committee, *Mankato: Its First Fifty Years*, 172–75; *Mankato Record*, March 29, 1862, April 19, 1863, May 5, 1866; *Mankato Independent*, March 31, 1862, April 23, 1863; *Mankato Review*, January 20, 1897.

21. Semi-centennial Committee, *Mankato: Its First Fifty Years*, 276–78.

22. Semi-centennial Committee, *Mankato: Its First Fifty Years*, 115–16, 276–78; von Festenberg-Pakisch and Schaub, *The History of SS. Peter and Paul's Parish*; Hughes, *History of Blue Earth County*, 174, 180.

23. Semi-centennial Committee, *Mankato: Its First Fifty Years*, 276–78.

24. Hughes, *History of Blue Earth County*, 125, 237.

25. Lause, *Secret Society History of the Civil War*, 1–37.

26. Bonthius, "The Patriot War of 1837–1838"; Kinchen, *Rise and Fall of the Patriot Hunters*; Lause, *Secret Society History of the Civil War*, 21–50.

27. For further reading on the role of filibuster expeditions and secret societies in Manifest Destiny and the US Civil War, see de la Cova, "Filibusters and Freemasons"; Keehn, *Knights of the Golden Circle*; Klement, *Dark Lanterns*; Lause, *Secret Society History of the Civil War*; May, *Manifest Destiny's Underworld*; and Owsley and Smith, *Filibusters and Expansionists*.

28. Lause, *Secret Society History of the Civil War*, 51–66.

29. Lause, *Secret Society History of the Civil War*, xiii, 152.

30. Lause, *Secret Society History of the Civil War*, 62.

31. Lause, *Secret Society History of the Civil War*, 152.

32. Schloff, "Overcoming Geography," 3n2, 4, 8; Lass, "Ginseng Rush in Minnesota."

33. Hughes, *History of Blue Earth County*, 138, 311–622.

34. John J. Porter to Henry Rice, November 17, 1861, John J. Porter to William P. Dole, June 8, 1863–both Letters Received, Winnebago

Agency, reel 935, 936; Porter wrote reference letters for Asa White in 1861 and 1863. Chapman, *History of Mankato Lodge No. 12*, 7.

35. *Mankato Record*, October 7, 1862; "Removal of the Winnebago Indians," petition; *St. Paul Daily Globe*, November 11, 1880.

Notes to Chapter 7: The Knights of the Forest

1. US Senate, *Reports . . . for the First Session of the Fiftieth Congress, 1887–88, Committee on Pensions, Report No.* 2282; Chapman, *History of Mankato Lodge No. 12*, 25; *Mankato Daily Free Press*, May 4, 1926.

2. *Mankato Review*, April 27, 1886; Hughes, *History of Blue Earth County*, 138; the reference to "Meridan" may have been a typo for Meriden, in Steele County.

3. *Mankato Review*, April 27, 1886; *Mankato Daily Review*, April 18, 1916; *Mankato Free Press*, July 23, 1896.

4. Semi-centennial Committee, *Mankato: Its First Fifty Years*, 95; Minnesota Geospatial Information Office, General Land Office Historic Plat Map Retrieval System (original plat maps); US Department of the Interior Bureau of Land Management General Land Office Records, Land Patent Documents (original land patents).

5. "Removal of the Winnebago Indians," petition. On Guy K. Cleveland, see Kiester, "The Bench and Bar of Faribault County," 60; "Local History Items," *Minnesota History* 13, no. 2 (June 1932): 214.

6. *Mankato Review*, April 27, 1886.

7. *Mankato Review*, April 27, 1886.

8. Sorensen, "Press Coverage of the Dakota Conflict of 1862," 101, 106.

9. Lass, "Removal from Minnesota," 353; *Mankato Record*, November 8, 1862, January 17, 1863.

10. "Removal of the Winnebago Indians," petition; Semi-centennial Committee, *Mankato: Its First Fifty Years*, 115, 156, 188–94; Hughes, *History of Blue Earth County*, 102.

11. "Removal of the Winnebago Indians," petition.

12. "Ritual/Initiation, Grand Lodge of the Knights of the Forest."

13. *Mankato Daily Review*, April 18, 1916.

14. "Ritual/Initiation, Grand Lodge of the Knights of the Forest."

15. "Ritual/Initiation, Grand Lodge of the Knights of the Forest."

16. *Mankato Review*, April 27, 1886; *Mankato Daily Review*, April 18, 1916.

17. *Report of the Commissioner of Indian Affairs for the Year 1862*, 236.

18. *Report of the Commissioner of Indian Affairs for the Year 1862*, 236.

19. *Report of the Commissioner of Indian Affairs for the Year 1862*, 236–37; John G. Morrison's testimony, 1911, in "Documents of an Investigation of the White Earth Reservation," Records of the Department of the Interior, Commissioner of Indian Affairs, Classified Files: White Earth 83129–1911–211, National Archives, as quoted in Treuer, *The Assassination of Hole in the Day*, 145.

20. Hughes, *History of Blue Earth County*, 125, 237.

21. Hughes, *History of Blue Earth County*, 93; Hughes, *Indian Chiefs of Southern Minnesota*, 180. "That the Indian had no rights" is paraphrased from the 1857 Dred Scott decision.

22. Minnesota Board of Commissioners, *Minnesota in the Civil and Indian Wars*, 1:455–57; Noyes, "Neighbors 'to the Rescue.'"

23. *Mankato Review*, April 27, 1886; *Mankato Daily Review*, April 18, 1916.

24. Griswold, *Mankato and Blue Earth County*, 5.

25. "Removal of the Winnebago Indians," petition.

26. *Winnebago Tribe of Indians vs. the United States of America, No. M-421: Petition of the Winnebago Tribe of Indians*; *Mankato Record*, May 16 and 23, 1863; Hughes, *Indian Chiefs of Southern Minnesota*, 178; Kantrowitz, *Citizens of a Stolen Land*, 99; Lass, "Removal from Minnesota," 362.

27. As quoted in Diedrich, *Winnebago Oratory*, 92.

Notes to Chapter 8:
The Banishment of the Ho-Chunk from Minnesota

1. *Report of the Commissioner of Indian Affairs for the Year 1862*; Alexander Ramsey to Caleb B. Smith, August 30, 1862, Henry Sibley to John Palmer Usher, January 19, 1863 – both Letters Received, Winnebago Agency, reel 936; Lass, "Removal from Minnesota," 354.

2. *Report of the Commissioner of Indian Affairs for the Year 1862*,

237; Hughes, *History of Blue Earth County*, 138–39; *Mankato Record*, October 4, 1862; Waggoner, "Sibley's Winnebago Prisoners," 34.

3. *Winona Daily Republican*, May 18, 1863.

4. S. F. Balcombe to William P. Dole, Letters Received, Winnebago Agency, reel 936.

5. Letters to Clark W. Thompson from S. F. Balcombe, John J. Porter, and Asa White, August 3 and November 9 and 17, 1860, March 10, 1861—all Letters Received, Winnebago Agency, reel 936; *Mankato Semi-Weekly Record*, October 25, 1862; Hughes, *History of Blue Earth County*, 139.

6. Anderson, *Massacre in Minnesota*, 73; S. F. Balcombe to William P. Dole, May 12, 1863, Letters Received, Winnebago Agency, reel 936. See also Nichols, *Lincoln and the Indians*. John J. Porter and "Madam White" wrote letters to the Office of Indian Affairs in the spring of 1863 to request that she be allowed to keep her 1859 allotment; see Madam White to William P. Dole and John J. Porter to William P. Dole, June 8, 1863. The request was evidently successful. Asa White died at his farm "at the old Winnebago Agency" in 1880: *St. Paul Daily Globe*, November 11, 1880.

7. "Ratified Treaty No. 310"; *Mankato Independent*, February 20, 1863; Hughes, *History of Blue Earth County*, 139; Lass, "Removal from Minnesota," 361.

8. *Mankato Record*, May 2, 9, 16, 1863; *Mankato Independent*, May 15, 1863.

9. *Report of the Commissioner of Indian Affairs for the Year 1863*, 312; Hughes, *History of Blue Earth County*, 139; *Mankato Record*, May 16, 23, 1863.

10. *St. Paul Weekly Press*, May 14–15, 21, 1863; *St. Paul Pioneer*, May 14, 1863.

11. Hughes, *Indian Chiefs of Southern Minnesota*, 179–81; interview notes from John Blackhawk, Hughes, Thomas, and Family Papers, Minnesota State University, Mankato; Minnesota Board of Commissioners, *Minnesota in the Civil and Indian Wars*, 1:455–57.

12. Hyman, "Survival at Crow Creek," 155.

13. Hyman, "Survival at Crow Creek"; Lass, "The 'Moscow Expedition'"; Lonetree, "Visualizing Native Survivance," 19.

14. Bieder, *Native American Communities in Wisconsin*, 171; *Visions and Voices: Winnebago Elders Speak to the Children*.

15. Henry Sibley to John Palmer Usher, January 19, 1963, Henry Sibley to Robert Oliver Selfridge, May 23, 1863–both Letters Received, Winnebago Agency, reel 936.

16. *Mankato Independent*, May 15, 1863.

17. *Mankato Review*, April 27, 1886.

Notes to Chapter 9:
Ethnic Cleansing and the Forgotten Legacy

1. Flint, ed., *Spaces of Hate*, 251; Anderson, *Conquest of Texas*, 7.

2. Anderson, *Conquest of Texas*, 7.

3. Browning, *Ordinary Men*.

4. Hughes, *History of Blue Earth County*, 141; Semi-centennial Committee, *Mankato: Its First Fifty Years*, 95.

5. *Mankato Free Press*, January 24, 2006.

6. Flint, ed., *Spaces of Hate*, 251.

7. *Mankato Daily Review*, April 18, 1916.

8. *Mankato Review*, April 27, 1886.

BIBLIOGRAPHY

Primary Sources

Chapman, Charles. Journals, 1856–57, 1876. Blue Earth County Historical Society, Mankato.

Commissioner of Indian Affairs. Department of the Interior. Classified Files: White Earth 83129–1911–211. National Archives. Available as: "Records of Investigation of White Earth Mixed Bloods, 1911–1915," M R 444. Minnesota Historical Society, St. Paul.

"Documents Relating to the Negotiation of Ratified and Unratified Treaties with Various Tribes of Indians, 1801–1869." Record Group 75, Bureau of Indian Affairs, National Archives. Available online: University of Wisconsin–Madison Libraries, http://digital.library.wisc.edu/1711.dl/S7IPANGUTYOW48J.

Hughes, Thomas, 1854–1934, and Family Papers, 1855–1946. Manuscript Collection 101. Southern Minnesota Historical Center. Minnesota State University, Mankato.

Message of Governor Ramsey to the Legislature of Minnesota, Delivered September 9, 1862. St. Paul, MN: Wm. R. Marshall, State Printer, 1862.

Minnesota Geospatial Information Office. General Land Office Historic Plat Map Retrieval System.

Minnesota People Records Search. Minnesota Historical Society. www.mnhs.org/search/people.

Old Main Cornerstone Collection, 1869–1969. University Archives, Minnesota State University, Mankato.

Records of the Internal Revenue Service. M774. Record Group 58, National Archives.

Reports of the Commissioner of Indian Affairs. Washington, DC: Government Printing Office.

US Department of the Interior. Bureau of Land Management. General Land Office Records, Land Patent Documents.

US Office of Indian Affairs. Letters Received by the Office of Indian Affairs, 1824–1880. Winnebago Agency, 1826–1875. Record Group 75, Records of the Office of Indian Affairs, National Archives.

US Senate. *Reports of Committees of the Senate of the United States for the First Session of the Fiftieth Congress, 1887–88. Committee on Pensions. Report No. 2282.* Washington, DC: Government Printing Office, 1888.

Winnebago Tribe of Indians, Plaintiffs, vs. the United States of America, Defendant, No. M-421: Petition of the Winnebago Tribe of Indians. Filed 3rd Day of December, 1931. Washington, DC[?], 1931.

NEWSPAPERS

Chicago Daily Tribune
College Reporter
Grange Advance (Red Wing)
Irish Standard (Minneapolis)
Litchfield Independent Review
Madison Democrat
Mankato Daily Free Press
Mankato Daily Review
Mankato Free Press
Mankato Independent
Mankato Record
Mankato Review
Mankato Semi-Weekly Record
Mankato Union
Mankato Weekly Record
Mankato Weekly Review
St. Cloud Times
St. Paul Daily Globe
St. Paul Pioneer
St. Paul Weekly Press

Secondary Sources

Anderson, Gary Clayton. *The Conquest of Texas: Ethnic Cleansing in the Promised Land, 1820–1875*. Norman: University of Oklahoma Press, 2005.

———. *Little Crow: Spokesman for the Sioux*. St. Paul: Minnesota Historical Society Press, 1986.

———. *Massacre in Minnesota: The Dakota War of 1862, the Most Violent Ethnic Conflict in American History*. Norman: University of Oklahoma Press, 2019.

Anderson, Gary Clayton, and Alan R. Woolworth, eds. *Through Dakota Eyes: Narrative Accounts of the Minnesota Indian War of 1862*. St. Paul: Minnesota Historical Society Press, 1988.

Bachman, Walt. "Colonel Miller's War." In *Trails of Tears: Minnesota's Dakota Indian Exile Begins*, edited by Mary Hawker Bakeman and Antona Hawkins Richardson, 107–22. Roseville, MN: Prairie Echoes, Park Genealogical Books, 2008.

———. *Northern Slave, Black Dakota: The Life and Times of Joseph Godfrey*. Bloomington, MN: Pond Dakota Press, 2013.

Bakeman, Mary Hawker, and Antona Hawkins Richardson, eds. *Trails of Tears: Minnesota's Dakota Indian Exile Begins*. Roseville, MN: Prairie Echoes, Park Genealogical Books, 2008.

Bieder, Robert E. *Native American Communities in Wisconsin, 1600–1960: A Study of Tradition and Change*. Madison: University of Wisconsin Press, 1995.

Bonthius, Andrew. "The Patriot War of 1837–1838: Locofocoism with a Gun?" *Labour / Le Travail* 52 (Fall 2003): 9–43.

Brown, Dee Alexander. *Bury My Heart at Wounded Knee: An Indian History of the American West*. New York: Holt, Rinehart and Winston, 1971.

Browning, Christopher. *Ordinary Men: Reserve Police Battalion 101 and the Final Solution in Poland*. New York: HarperCollins, 1992.

Canku, Clifford, and Michael Simon, with John Peacock. *The Dakota Prisoner of War Letters: Dakota Kaskapi Okicize Wowapi*. St. Paul: Minnesota Historical Society Press, 2013.

Case, Martin. *The Relentless Business of Treaties: How Indigenous Land Became US Property*. St. Paul: Minnesota Historical Society Press, 2018.

Cavanagh, Edward, and Lorenzo Veracini, eds. *The Routledge Handbook of the History of Settler Colonialism*. New York: Routledge, 2017.

Chapman, Charles A. *History of Mankato Lodge No. 12*. Mankato, MN: Free Press Print, 1902.

——. *Mankato and Blue Earth County, Minnesota, A Historical and Descriptive Sketch with the Fifth Annual Report of the Board of Trade of the City of Mankato, Minnesota, for the Year 1877*. Mankato, MN: Wise and Coffin, 1878.

Chatelain, Verne E. "The Federal Land Policy and Minnesota Politics, 1854–60." *Minnesota History* 22, no. 3 (September 1941): 227–48.

Chomsky, Carol. "The United States–Dakota War Trials: A Study in Military Justice." *Stanford Law Review* 43, no. 1 (November 1990): 13–98.

de la Cova, Antonio Rafael. "Filibusters and Freemasons: The Sworn Obligation." *Journal of the Early Republic* 17, no. 1 (Spring 1997): 95–120.

De La Ronde, John. "Personal Narrative." *Collections of the Wisconsin State Historical Society* 7 (1908): 345–65.

Diedrich, Mark. *Winnebago Oratory: Great Moments in the Recorded Speech of the Hochungra, 1742–1887*. Rochester, MN: Coyote Books, 1991.

Edmunds, R. David, ed. *American Indian Leaders: Studies in Diversity*. Lincoln: University of Nebraska Press, 1980.

——. *Enduring Nations: Native Americans in the Midwest*. Urbana: University of Illinois Press, 2008.

Flint, Colin, ed. *Spaces of Hate: Geographies of Discrimination and Intolerance in the U.S.A.* New York: Routledge, 2003.

Folwell, William Watts. *A History of Minnesota*. 4 vols. St. Paul: Minnesota Historical Society, 1921.

Griswold, William B. *Mankato and Blue Earth County: A Brief Review of the Past, Present, and Future of the City . . .* Mankato: Griswold and Neff, 1867.

Hall, John W. *Uncommon Defense: Indian Allies in the Black Hawk War*. Cambridge, MA: Harvard University Press, 2009.

Harstad, Peter T. "Disease and Sickness on the Wisconsin Frontier: Smallpox and Other Diseases." *Wisconsin Magazine of History* 43, no. 4 (Summer 1960): 253–63.

Hixson, Walter L. "Adaptation, Resistance and Representation in the Modern US Settler State." In *The Routledge Handbook of the History of Settler Colonialism*, edited by Edward Cavanagh and Lorenzo Veracini. New York: Routledge, 2017.

Hubbard. L. F., and R. I. Holcombe. *Minnesota in Three Centuries, 1655–1908*. 4 vols. New York: Publishing Society of Minnesota, 1908.

Hughes, Thomas. *History of Blue Earth County and Biographies of Its Leading Citizens*. Chicago: Middle West Publishing Company, 1901. http://www.archive.org/details/cu31924028912925.

——. *Indian Chiefs of Southern Minnesota: Containing Sketches of the Prominent Chieftains of the Dakota and Winnebago Tribes from 1825 to 1865*. 2nd ed. Minneapolis: Ross and Haines, 1969.

Hyman, Collette. *Dakota Women's Work: Creativity, Culture, and Exile*. St. Paul: Minnesota Historical Society Press, 2012.

——. "Survival at Crow Creek, 1863–1866." *Minnesota History* 61, no. 4 (Winter 2008): 148–61.

Jarvis, William. *Time Capsules: A Cultural History*. Jefferson, NC: McFarland, 2003.

Jorstad, Erling. "Personal Politics in the Origin of Minnesota's Democratic Party." *Minnesota History* 36, no. 7 (September 1959): 259–71.

Kantrowitz, Stephen. *Citizens of a Stolen Land: A Ho-Chunk History of the Nineteenth-Century United States*. Chapel Hill: University of North Carolina Press, 2023.

Kappler, Charles, ed. *Indian Affairs: Laws and Treaties. Vol. II (Treaties)*. Washington, DC: Government Printing Office, 1904.

Keehn, David C. *Knights of the Golden Circle: Secret Empire, Southern Secession, Civil War*. Baton Rouge: Louisiana State University Press, 2013.

Kiester, J. A. "The Bench and Bar of Faribault County" (1896–1904). Minnesota Legal History Project: minnesotalegalhistoryproject .org.

Kinchen, Oscar. *The Rise and Fall of the Patriot Hunters*. New York: Bookman Associates, 1956.

Klement, Frank L. *Dark Lanterns: Secret Political Societies, Conspiracies, and Treason Trials in the Civil War*. Baton Rouge: Louisiana State University Press, 1984.

Lass, William E. "Ginseng Rush in Minnesota." *Minnesota History* 41, no. 6 (Summer 1969): 249–66.

——. "The 'Moscow Expedition.'" *Minnesota History* 39, no. 6 (Summer 1965): 227–40.

——. "The Removal from Minnesota of the Sioux and Winnebago Indians." *Minnesota History* 38, no. 8 (December 1963): 353–64.

Lause, Mark. *A Secret Society History of the Civil War.* Urbana: University of Illinois Press, 2011.

Loew, Patty. *Indian Nations of Wisconsin: Histories of Endurance and Renewal.* Madison: Wisconsin Historical Society Press, 2013.

Lonetree, Amy. "Visualizing Native Survivance: Encounters with My Ho-Chunk Ancestors in the Family Photographs of Charles Van Schaick." In *People of the Big Voice: Photographs of Ho-Chunk Families by Charles Van Schaick, 1879–1942.* Madison: Wisconsin Historical Society Press, 2011.

Lurie, Nancy. "The Winnebago Indians: A Study in Cultural Change." PhD diss., Northwestern University, 1952.

——. *Wisconsin Indians.* Rev. ed. Madison: Wisconsin Historical Society Press, 2002.

May, Robert E. *Manifest Destiny's Underworld: Filibustering in Antebellum America.* Chapel Hill: University of North Carolina Press, 2002.

McBride, Genevieve G. *Women's Wisconsin: From Native Matriarchies to the New Millennium.* Madison: Wisconsin Historical Society Press, 2005.

Minnesota Board of Commissioners. *Minnesota in the Civil and Indian Wars 1861–1865.* 2 vols. St. Paul, MN: Pioneer Press, 1890.

Monjeau-Marz, Corinne L. *The Dakota Indian Internment at Fort Snelling, 1862–1864.* St. Paul, MN: Prairie Smoke Press, 2006.

Murphy, Lucy Eldersveld. "Autonomy and the Economic Roles of Indian Women of the Fox-Wisconsin Riverway Region, 1763–1832." In *Negotiators of Change: Historical Perspectives on Native American Women,* edited by Nancy Shoemaker. New York: Routledge, 1995.

——. "'Their Women Quite Industrious Miners': Native American Lead Mining in the Upper Mississippi Valley, 1788–1832." In *Enduring Nations: Native Americans in the Midwest,* edited by R. David Edmunds, 36–53. Urbana: University of Illinois Press, 2008.

Nichols, David A. *Lincoln and the Indians: Civil War Policy and Politics.* 1978. Reprint, St. Paul: Minnesota Historical Society Press, 2012.

Noyes, Edward. "Neighbors 'to the Rescue': Wisconsin and Iowa Troops Fight Boredom, Not Indians, in Minnesota in 1862." *Minnesota History* 46, no. 8 (Winter 1979): 312–27.

Ostler, Jeffrey. *Surviving Genocide: Native Nations and the United States from the American Revolution to Bleeding Kansas.* New Haven, CT: Yale University Press, 2019.

Owsley, Frank Lawrence, and Gene A. Smith. *Filibusters and Expansionists: Jeffersonian Manifest Destiny, 1800–1821.* Tuscaloosa: University of Alabama Press, 1997.

Peterson, Teresa R., and Walter LaBatte. *Voices from Pejuhutazizi: Dakota Stories and Storytellers.* St. Paul: Minnesota Historical Society Press, 2022.

Pluth, Edward. "Account of Winnebago Affairs at Long Prairie, Minnesota Territory, 1848–1855." Master's thesis, St. Cloud State University, 1963.

———. "The Failed Watab Treaty of 1853." *Minnesota History* 57, no. 1 (Spring 2000): 2–22.

Quaife, M. M. "The Panic of 1862 in Wisconsin." *Wisconsin Magazine of History* 4, no. 2 (December 1920): 166–95.

Radin, Paul. *The Winnebago Tribe.* 1923. Reprint, Lincoln: University of Nebraska Press, 1970.

Rayman, Ronald A. "Confrontation at the Fever River Lead Mining District: Joseph Montfort Street vs. Henry Dodge, 1827–28." *Annals of Iowa* 44, no. 4 (Spring 1978): 278–95.

Richards, Patricia. "Winnebago Subsistence: Change and Continuity." *Wisconsin Archeologist* 74, no. 1–4 (1993): 272–89.

Routel, Colette. "Minnesota Bounties on Dakota Men during the US–Dakota War." *William Mitchell Law Review* 40 (2013).

Schloff, Linda Mack. "Overcoming Geography: Jewish Religious Life in Four Market Towns." *Minnesota History* 51, no. 1 (Spring 1988): 2–14.

Semi-centennial Committee on Publications. *Mankato: Its First Fifty Years.* Mankato: Free Press Printing, 1903.

Shoemaker, Nancy, ed. *Negotiators of Change: Historical Perspectives on Native American Women.* New York: Routledge, 1995.

Shrake, Peter. "Chasing an Elusive War: The Illinois Militia and the Winnebago War of 1827." *Journal of Illinois History* 12, no. 1 (Spring 2009): 8–50.

Smith, David Lee. "Ho-Chunk Tribal History: The History of the Ho-Chunk People from the Mound Building Era to the Present Day." [N.p.: n.p,] 1996.

Sorensen, David M. "Press Coverage of the Dakota Conflict of 1862." Master's thesis, St. Cloud State University, 2005.

Spector, Janet. "Winnebago Indians, 1634–1829: An Archeological and Ethnohistoric Investigation." PhD diss., University of Wisconsin, 1974.

Treaties between the Winnebago Indians and the United States of America, 1817–1856. Museum of Anthropology Miscellaneous Series, vol. 1. Greeley: Colorado State College, 1967.

Treuer, Anton. *The Assassination of Hole in the Day.* St. Paul, MN: Borealis Books, 2011.

Visions and Voices: Winnebago Elders Speak to the Children. Independence, WI: Western Dairyland Economic Opportunity Council, 1994.

von Festenberg-Pakisch, Wilhelm, and Arthur Schaub. *The History of SS. Peter and Paul's Parish in Mankato, Minnesota, 1854–1899.* Mankato, MN: S. S. Peter and Paul Heritage Committee, 1999.

Waggoner, L. M. "Sibley's Winnebago Prisoners: Deconstructing Race and Recovering Kinship in the Dakota War of 1862." *Great Plains Quarterly* 33, no. 1 (January 2013): 25–48.

Waziyatawin (Angela Wilson). *What Does Justice Look Like? The Struggle for Liberation in Dakota Homeland.* St. Paul, MN: Living Justice Press, 2008.

Westerman, Gwen, and Bruce M. White. *Mni Sota Makoce: The Land of the Dakota.* St. Paul: Minnesota Historical Society Press, 2012.

White, Bruce M. "Indian Visits: Stereotypes of Minnesota's Native People." *Minnesota History* 53, no. 3 (Fall 1992): 99–111.

———. "The Power of Whiteness: Or, the Life and Times of Joseph Rolette Jr." *Minnesota History* 56, no. 4 (Winter 1998): 178–97.

Willard, John A. *Blue Earth County: Its Advantages to Settlers.* Mankato, MN: John C. Wise "Record" Office, 1868.

Wingerd, Mary Lethert. *North Country: The Making of Minnesota.* Minneapolis: University of Minnesota Press, 2010.

Zanger, Martin. "Red Bird." In *American Indian Leaders: Studies in Diversity,* edited by R. David Edmunds. Lincoln: University of Nebraska Press, 1980.

INDEX

Page numbers in *italic* refer to images or captions.

Acton, 48
Algonquin language, 9
Anderson, Gary Clayton, 108–9
Apache, 108
Ardent Mills, 101
assimilation, forced, 28, 30
Atkinson, Henry, 14

Balcombe, Saint Andre Durand, 48–49, *93*, 97, 99; accusations of corruption, 99–100; annual report, 95–96
Barney, Asa, 3, 57, 65–69, 71, 74, 81, 85–86; birth, 65; membership in Knights of the Forest, *66*, 67, 69, 83; obituary, 81; portrait of, *66*; purchase of Ho-Chunk lands, 67, 83, 111
Barney, Charles, 65–66, 71, 74
Barney, Sheldon F., 2–3, 65–69, 71, 74, 85–86; ad distributed by, *68*; in the Mankato Home Guards, 73; membership in Knights of the Forest, *66*, 67, 69, 83; move to Minnesota, 65; portrait of, *66*; purchase of Ho-Chunk lands, 67, 83, 95, 111
Battle of New Ulm, 63, 71–72, 74
Bdote, 35
Bear clan, 23
Bickley, George, 76–77
Birch Coulee, 49
Black Hawk War, 20, 40
Black River, 23
Black River Falls, 10, 115, *116*
Blackhawk, John, 103
Blue Earth County, 20, 42, 53, 60, 62, 71, 78, 82, 86, 107, 111; Ho-Chunk reservation in, 3–4, 7, 26, 32–34, 38–40, 42–48, 55, 56, 61–62, 73, 78–79, 83–85, 93–100, 102, 106, 112–13; Ho-Chunk reservation, allotments, 39–40, 44; petition to Lincoln from, 83–86, 95; survey of, 57, 59; violence at, 93–97
Blue Earth River, 4, 39
the Boxer, 13
British, 11, 35
Brotherhood of the Union, 75
Brown, Orlando, 30, 31

Brown County, 5, 50, 55, 86; Dakota in, 4
Browning, Christopher, 110
Buchanan, James, 62
Buck, Daniel, 86–88
Burgess, Harvey, 88
Burns, John, 42, 61
Butter, Reuben, 88

Calhoun, James C., 13
Camp Porter, 63, 65, 81, 96, 101–2
Caramonee, 12
Case, Martin, 28
Cass, Lewis, 13–14
Chapman, Charles A., Jr., 3, 57–62, 65, 71, 81, 83, 85–87, 94; advocation of Ho-Chunk removal, 61–62, 95, 109, 111–12; birth, 57; death, 92; education, 57; Knights of the Forest membership, 58, 60, 69, 79, 88, 90–91, 109; in the Mankato Home Guards, 73; portrait, 58; surveying business, 57, 59, 87
Charles Chapman House, 59
Chou-Ga-Ga, 105
Citizens' National Bank, 72, 86, 87
Cleveland, Guy K., 83
College Reporter, 1
Comanche, 108
Committee of Safety, 13, 74
Company One, Tenth Regiment of Minnesota, 103
The Conquest of Texas: Ethnic Cleansing in the Promised Land, 1820–1875 (Anderson), 108
Cray, Lorin, 88
Crow Creek Reservation, 96, 100, 102–4, 106

Daily Review: "Secret Society of Early Mankato," 60, 88, 90
Dakota, 7, 12–13, 23, 30, 106, 109, 111; annuities, 36, 48; in Blue Earth County, 34, 36, 113; in Brown County, 4; conflicts with settler-colonists, 48–49, 50, 90; credit, 48; debt owed to, 48; execution, reconciliation/commemoration of, 112; farming, 36; hangings, 150th anniversary of, 112; hunting, 36; internment at Fort Snelling, 4, 51–52, 95; mass execution of, 3–5, 49–50, 52–57, 69, 81, 94–95, 101, 113; Mdewakanton, 35–36, 48; of Minnesota, 115; origin stories, 35; removal of, 4, 36, 50–51, 55–57, 82, 98, 104; reservation at Crow Creek, SD, 104; Sisseton, 36; traditional territory, 35; Wahpekute, 36; Wahpeton, 36, war with United States, 7, 34, 61–62, 64, 66, 69, 71–73, 78–79, 85, 92–94, 96, 99, 108–9, 111–13
Danville, 42
Danville Home Guards, 74
Decora, Waukon, 15, 18, 20, 40
Democrats, 47, 85, 87–88, 100
Dodge, Henry, 13–14, 16, 17, 24; Committee of Safety, 13, 74
Dowlin, Bruce, 112
Dowlin, Sheryl, 112
Dubuque, Julien, 11

Edgerton, Alonzo, 94
Emancipation Proclamation, 82
epidemics, 9–10; smallpox, 23
ethnic cleansing/genocide of Indigenous peoples, 4–5, 7; forgotten legacy of, 107–16; state sanctioned efforts, 4

Fairchild, Lucius, *105*
Faribault County, 83
Favorite, *102*
*Fifth Annual Report of the Board of
    Trade of the City of Mankato,
    Minnesota* (Chapman), 60
First National Bank of Mankato,
    72, 86
Flint, Colin, 108
Fort Crawford, 16
Fort Ridgely, 49
Fort Snelling, 4, 13; Dakota interred
    at, 4, 51–52, 95; Ho-Chunk
    interred at, *43, 102, 103*
Franklin, Benjamin, 65
Freemasons, 74–76, 78
French, 10, 11, 35
Frontier Rangers, 63–64

Galena, 13, 14
Garden City, 60, 61, 67, 69, 74, 82
German Police Battalion 101, 110
ginseng, 44, 78, 97
Gorman, Willis, 32
Grand Army of the Republic Hall, 2
Great Famine, 70
Green Bay, 9–10

Harvard University, 57, 83
hate groups, 7, 109; geographic
    explanation of, 108
Henderson, 51
*History of Blue Earth County and
    Biography of Its Leading Citizens*
    (Hughes), 46, 67
History of Masonic Lodge No. 12
    (Chapman), 60
Hitler, Adolf, 110
Ho-Chunk Nation, 3, 7, 67, 83,
    113–15; Agency, 74, 78; agricul-
    ture, 10, 44, 94–95, 97; alcohol
    and, 46–47; annuities, 39,
48, 83, 85; army protection of,
    49; cessions, removals, and
    reservations, 6, 22, 35, 39–40;
    claims filed, 95–96; conflicts
    with Dakota, 49; conflicts with
    settler-colonists, 46–48; debt
    owed to, 40–41, 48; disease and,
    10, 23; District 4, 115; gender
    divisions, 10–11; hunting, 11–12,
    19; interred at Camp Porter,
    101–2; interred at Fort Snelling,
    43, 102, 103; land allotments,
    39–40, 44, 98; land exchanges,
    32, 34; lead mines, 10–13, 15–17,
    19–20, 35; paramilitary activity
    around reservation, 74; pen-
    sions, 20; population in 1634, 9;
    population in 1834, 23; purchase
    of Omaha Reservation, 104;
    racial imagery used to vilify,
    110–11; reconciliation/com-
    memoration of, 112; removal
    from Minnesota, 64–65, 81, 83,
    95, 97–106, 108, 110–12; removal
    from Minnesota, advocating
    for, 3–4, 42–48, 55–56, 61–63,
    82–86, 91–92, 107–9, 111;
    removal from Wisconsin, 7,
    23–26, 105; requests for new res-
    ervation land, 32; reservation in
    Blue Earth County, 3–4, 7, 26,
    32–34, 36–40, 44–48, 55–56,
    61–62, 73, 78–79, 93–100, 102,
    106, 112–13; reservation in Crow
    Creek, SD, 98–100, *102*, 102–4,
    106; reservation in Long Prairie,
    28–32, 34, 106; reservation in
    Nebraska, 64; reservation in
    the Neutral Ground, 23–26;
    resistance to removal from
    Minnesota, 102; resistance to
    removal from Wisconsin, 24,

26, 30, 50, 99, 104–5, 115; starvation, 97–98; threats to, 93–98; trade with, 10–11, 27, 44, 47, 78, 100; traditional territory, 9–10, 12, 14, 19–26, 35, 96, 99, 104–6, 115; treaties, 10–12, 15–16, 19–23, 32–33, 35, 37, 39–40, 42–43, 98; tribal annuities, 24, 27; white settlers on land, 11–26, 37, 39, 111
Ho-Chunk Nation of Wisconsin, 115
Hochungra (People of the Big Voice/People of the Sacred Language), 9
Hole in the Day, 93
Holocaust, 110
Hopokoekau/Glory of the Morning, 10
Houston County, 115
Hubbard Mill, 101
Hughes, Thomas, 37, 42, 45–46, 57, 62, 65, 67, 69, 73, 78–79, 82, 88, 94, 98–99, 103
Hunters Lodges, 75

Illinois, 115
Independent Order of Odd Fellows, 2, 69, 78
Indian Wars, 109
International Hotel, 65
Iowa Territory, 20, 23–26

Kickapoo River, 23
Kiowa, 108
Knights of Columbus, 75
Knights of the Forest, *58*, 60, 64–65, 71–73, 79, 81–96, 107, 111, 116; campaign against Ho-Chunk, 7, 56–57, 61–63, 79, 82–83, 85–86, 90–91, 95, 100, 106–10, 112; cornerstone ceremony (1869), 3; fire, 83; Grand Lodge, 60, 74,

88, 94, 109; initiation rites, 1, 3–4, 56–57, 60, 82–83, 90–91; leadership/founding members, 60, 66–67, 69, 85–88, 108; oath, 1, 3–4, 83, 85, 88, 90–91, 94–95, 110; purchase of Ho-Chunk land, 42; recruitment techniques, 88–89; "Ritual," 1, 3, 56–57, 61, 69, 82, 88, *89*, 91, 95, 113; secrecy, 91–92, 95, 106
Knights of the Golden Circle, 76–77
Knights Templar, 69
Ku Klux Klan, 91, 107

La Crosse, 12
Lake Elysian, 96, 102
Lake Michigan, 15
LaSallier, Baptiste, 40, 42, 96
Lause, Mark, 74–78
Le Crescent, 115
Lincoln, Abraham, 49, 51–52, 54, 62, 81–82, 100; petition sent to, 83–86, 95
Little Crow, 35, 48
Little Elk, 17
Little Priest, 20
Lonetree, Amy, 20, 104
Long Prairie reservation, 28–32, 34, 106; lumber on, 33; purpose of, 30–32
Lower Sioux Agency, 48
Lucero, Linda, *116*

Madelia, 64
Mahkato, 34
Manifest Destiny, 4, 7, 75–76, 107
Mankato, 27, 42, 87, 92, 110–11; bird's-eye view of, *5*; Blue Earth bridge, 52–54; charter, 39; Dakota prisoners at, 49–50, 52–54, *56*, 57, 95; execution of

Dakota prisoners, 55, 69, 81, 94, 101, 112; Front Street, 1-2, *33, 59, 87*; growth, 78; marketing pamphlet, 95; martial law, 64; militia groups, 63-64, 71-73, 79, 93, 109; mob violence in, 5, 52-54, 94; population boom, 71; secret society tradition in, 55-79, 82, 112; trade with Ho-Chunk, 44

Mankato Artillery Company, 61

Mankato Free Press, 65

Mankato Home Guards, 63, 71, 73, 79, 93, 109

Mankato Independent, 71, 83, 86, 100, 106

Mankato: Its First Fifty Years, 66

Mankato Masons: Grand Lodge, 57, 64, 69, 70, 78-79, 81-82; Masonic Hall, 82; meetings, 81-82

Mankato Normal School, 1, 2; cornerstone, 1-2, 113; Old Main Building, 1, 2

Mankato Record, 71, 99

Mankato Review, 60, 61, 64, 86; "The Knights of the Forest: A Secret History," 60, 66, 82-83, 85-86, 92, 94-95, 106

Mankato State College, 1; Archives, 3; centennial, 2; cornerstone, 1-3; Old Main Building, 1-3; time capsule, 1-2, 69, 83

Mankato Union Office, *33*

Marks, Isaac, 79, 100

Marshall, William, 51

Mayo, William Worrall, 55

Mayo Clinic, 55

Meagher, John E., 3, 57, 63, 69-74, 81, 85-86, 111; birth, 70, 71; death, 72; as editor of the *Mankato Review*, 71; hardware store, 70-71; in the Mankato Home Guard, 73, 93; membership in Knights of the Forest, 70-73, 83, 88, 109

Menominee, 9, 14

Meriden, 60, 82

Meskwaki, 23

Michigan, 23, 75

militias, 77-78; home guard, 63, 71, 73, 74, 79, 93, 109; muster rolls, 73-74; state, 73

Miller, Stephen, 52-54

Minnesota: statehood, 39, 47; Territory, 12, 27-34, 57

Minnesota Land Office, 62

Minnesota River, 32, 35, 101, 102

Minnesota State Capitol, 2

Minnesota State Normal School Board, 86

Minnesota Supreme Court, 86

Minnesota Valley Railroad, 64

Minnetonka, 32, 37

Mississippi River, 12, 23, 32, 35, 93, 96-97

Missouri River, 27, 102, 104

Mni Sota Makoce, 35

Montevideo, 37

Moore, Marcus, 98

Moreland, Basil, *38*, 39

Myrick, Andrew, 48

National Citizens' Bank, 72

National Register of Historic Places, 59

Nazi Germany, 110

Nes-Ka-Ka/Whitewater, *105*

Neutral Ground, 23-26

New Ulm, 5, 49-50, 52, 55, 64; Battle of, 63, 71-72, 74

Nicollet, Jean, 9

Oceti Sakowiŋ/Seven Council Fires/
    Sioux, 35
O'-check-la/Four Legs, 14–15
Office of Indian Affairs, 32, 63, 83,
    97–99; corruption in, 99–100
Ohio, 75
Ojibwe, 12, 14, 28, 30, 50, 91, 95; of
    Minnesota, 115; traditional ter-
    ritory, 35; violence against, 93
Old Settlers Reunion, 67
Omaha, 27, 104
Omaha Reservation, 104
Order of the Lone Star, 77

Panic of 1857, 39
Patriot War, 75
Porter, Daniel, 63, 71, 74
Porter, E. D. B., 63–64, 71, 74, 88;
    embezzlement, charges of, 64;
    Knights of the Forest member-
    ship, 64, 86
Porter, Henry, 63, 71, 74
Porter, John H., Jr., 3, 57, 62–64, 71,
    74, 81; birth, 62; death, 62–63;
    Knights of the Forest member-
    ship, 62–64
Porter, John J., Sr., 3, 62, 63, 71, 74,
    81, 85; death, 64; Knights of
    the Forest membership, 63, 79,
    88, 106, 109; move to Mankato,
    62; political offices, 64–65, 88;
    sawmill, 62
Potawatomi, 9, 13
Prairie du Chien, 10, 13, 24

Ramsey, Alexander, 30–32, 49, 97,
    100, 111; call to remove Dakota
    from Minnesota, 50, 109;
    *Proclamation to the People of
    Minnesota*, 54
Reconciliation Park, 112

Red Banks, 9
Red Bird, 13–16, 19–20
Red Bird's Uprising, 13
Red Wing, 70
Reebok, *116*
Republicans, 47, 85, 87–88, 99–100
Rice, Henry Mower, 27, 29, 97, 100;
    contract to bring Ho-Chunk
    to Long Prairie, 28, 30; timber
    business, 33
Rice Lake, 46
Rochester, 55
Roman Catholic Church, 75

St. Cloud, 50
St. Cloud University, 2
St. Paul, 50, 64, 115
St. Paul and Sioux City Railroad
    Land Office, 64
St. Peter, 5, 52
St. Peter and Paul Catholic Church,
    72
Sauk, 20, 23
Scha-Chip-Ka-Ka, *105*
secret societies, 7, 69; American
    fraternal orders, 1–2, 74, 75,
    77–78; European freema-
    sonry, 74–75; labor groups, 75;
    in Mankato, 55–79; nine-
    teenth-century, 1–2, 4, 74–79;
    paramilitary groups, 4, 74, 79,
    91, 108–9; passwords, 74–75;
    political activity and, 74–79;
    propaganda created by, 77;
    racial terror and, 107–8; social
    web of, 77–78
*A Secret Society History of the Civil
    War* (Lause), 74
settler-colonialism, American, 11
Shelby, 74
Shelbyville, 62

Shrake, Peter, 14
Sibley, Henry Hastings, 27–30, 49, 52, 79, 106; treatment of Dakota, 51
Siouan language, 9, 104
slavery, 47, 76, 82
Sons of Liberty, 77
South Bend, 59, 87, 63
Spaces of Hate: Geographies of Discrimination and Intolerance in the U.S.A. (Flint), 108, 112
Spoon-De-Kaury/Spoon Decorah, *105, 115*
Spotted Arm, 19
Star Clothing House, 87
Steele County, *38*, 60
Street, Joseph, 16

Taylor, Zachary, 30
Tecumseh, 11
Texas, 108–9
Texas Rangers, 77, 108–9
Thompson, Clark, 44
Thunder clan, 10
treaty council of 1825, 12
Treaty of 1829, 20
Treaty of 1855, *19*
Treaty of 1859, 20, 40, 42–43, 98, 100
Treaty of 1865, *19*
Treaty of Fond de Lac, 28
Treaty of Mendota, 36
Treaty of Peace and Friendship, 12
Treaty of Prairie du Chien, 22, *115*
Treaty of Traverse des Sioux, 36
treaty payments, 30
treaty system, 28
Turkey River, 26
Tyner, Daniel, 53

Union of Brotherhood, 76
Universal Democratic Republicans, 75
Upper Sioux Agency, 48
US Civil War, 7, 47, 63, 75–76, 106–7, 109–11
US Congress, 47, 100
US–Dakota War, 7, 34, 66, 71–73, 78–79, 93, 96, 99; consequences for Dakota, 3–5, 49–50, 52–57, 69, 81, 94–95, 101, 113; consequences for Ho-Chunk, 61–65, 82–86, 91–92, 107–9, 111–12
US General Land Office, 67

Vernon, 74

Wa-So-Mo-Ne-Ka/Hail-stone, 105
Wakanjaxeriga/Roaring Thunder/ Dandy, 24–26, *105*
War of 1812, 11
Waseca County, *38*
Welliver, Daniel M., 112
Whig party, 30
Whipple, Josiah, 88
White, Asa, 79, 98–100
White, Bruce, 45–46
White Crow, 20
Wickersham, Moses, 64
Wilkinson, Morton S., 83, 85; bill to remove Ho-Chunk, 97–98; petition, 86–88, 111
Willard, John A., 66–67, 71, 86; ad distributed by, *68*
Winnebago, 9, 42, 49, 64, 82, 85, 92, 94; Nebraska Tribe of, 104, 115. *See also* Ho-Chunk Nation
Winnebago War, 13
Winneshiek/Coming Thunder, 20, 40, 42–44, 96, 98, 102; at Fort Snelling, *43, 103*

Winona, 12, *102*
Winona Daily Republican, 99
Wisconsin, 50, 74, 96, 99, 104–5, 115; Ho-Chunk Nation of, 115; statehood, 16, 23; Territory, 12–13, 16, 21, 23

Wise, John, 86
Wood Lake, 49

Yellow Thunder, 26, *105*
Yugoslavia, 109

To Banish Forever: A Secret Society, the Ho-Chunk, and Ethnic Cleansing in Minnesota was designed and set in type by Judy Gilats in St. Paul, Minnesota. The text face is Edita Small and the display faces are Gimlet Text Compressed and Program Narrow.